Praise for
The Happy Manifesto

'A book that makes the complex people stuff simple and straightforward. Anyone running any type of organization would benefit from *The Happy Manifesto*.'
Jane Sunley, CEO, learnpurple

'If only all organizations took the Happy approach, the workplaces of Britain would be far better places to work.'
Neil Currant, University of Salford

'The hierarchy of management needs is brilliant.'
Jonathan de Pass, Chief Executive, Evaluate Ltd

'This is not another book to read, enjoy and forget. You can apply the approach right after reading, and great results would be on your way. This book proves that management is not very complicated, all you have to do is to be more human and get the result.' **Waqas Ali, Hometown Shoes**

'The combination of 'Happy' stories, and the variety of examples from diverse industries makes it easy to see how I can tweak the ideas and implement them in my workplace.'
Lissy Thornquist, International Hotel Group

D0162268

If you want to build a thriving organization, start by creating a climate of freedom, support and stretch, in which your people feel energized and happy to give their best every day. Henry is a leader who creates this climate for success in his own organization, and a writer and speaker who inspires it in other organizations through his inspiring and achievable manifesto. I can't recommend him highly enough.
Alison Chadwick, BBDO Europe

Extremely inspirational. It has opened my eyes on different ways of working... **Paulina Latham, Polish Cultural Institute**

After reading *The Happy Manifesto*, I am scrapping my Masters thesis approach and adopting one inspired by your story. The stories, ideas and beliefs give me hope and evidence that we can change the nature of business for the good.
Todd Macdonald, Bmergent

So enthused was I by the Manifesto that I have taken it back into my own organization and begun to practice the Happy philosophy. My managers are equally enthusiastic and we are looking to use it as a vehicle for changing our organizational culture.
Stuart MacDonald, Norfolk and Suffolk Probation Trust

The Happy Manifesto offers simple, win-win advice, which has helped me personally balance the equation between financial and people performance across our portfolio of UK businesses.
Stuart Jones, Head of Customer Service, Carillion PLC

The Happy Manifesto has energized me and my business to make changes that have increased our bottom line and made people more successful and fulfilled at work. I used to be a busy Managing Director of 30 people, in the last 9 months I have increased my workforce to 50 people and I am less busy – fantastic! I carry *The Happy Manifesto* with me every day to work, it inspires me and challenges my ways of working. Thanks Henry!
Simon Perriton, Chief Executive, Just-IT

Customer Reviews

'Inspiring and energizing. I've had so many 'YES!' moments whilst reading it.' **Kerry Herbert**

'I feel that this book should be compulsory reading for all human resources managers; being happy brings out the highest potential for all of us.' **Pauline McDonald**

'The writing style made it a page turner for me. The questions at the end of each section prompted a clear next action.' **Andrew CR Westoby**

Thoroughly enjoyed *The Happy Manifesto*. Never thought I'd find a business/work-related book so gripping! **Kim George**

The Happy Manifesto

Make your organization a great workplace

HENRY STEWART

KoganPage

LONDON PHILADELPHIA NEW DELHI

First published in Great Britain in 2012 by Happy
This edition published in Great Britain and the United States in 2013 by Kogan Page Limited

120 Pentonville Road	1518 Walnut Street, Suite 1100	4737/23 Ansari Road
London N1 9JN	Philadelphia PA 19102	Daryaganj
United Kingdom	USA	New Delhi 110002
www.koganpage.com		India

© Henry Stewart 2012

The right of Henry Stewart to be identified as the author of this work has been asserted by him in accordance with the Copyright, Designs and Patents Act 1988.

ISBN   978 0 7494 6751 7
E-ISBN   978 0 7494 6752 4

British Library Cataloguing-in-Publication Data

A CIP record for this book is available from the British Library.

Library of Congress Cataloging-in-Publication Data

Stewart, Henry, 1959-
    The happy manifesto : make your organization a great workplace / Henry Stewart.
        p. cm.
    Includes index.
    ISBN 978-0-7494-6751-7 – ISBN 978-0-7494-6752-4 (ebook)   1. Work environment.
2. Job satisfaction.   3. Corporate culture.   4. Employee motivation.   I. Title.
    HD7261.S753 2013
    658.3'8–dc23   2012039395

Typeset by Graphicraft Limited, Hong Kong
Print production managed by Jellyfish
Printed and bound in the UK by CPI Group (UK) Ltd, Croydon, CR0 4YY

Contents

About Henry Stewart

Henry Stewart is Chief Executive of the training company Happy Ltd. Founded, as Happy Computers, in his back room in Hackney (east London) in 1988, it now trains 20,000 people a year and has received widespread recognition. The company has been rated:

- best company in the UK for customer service (*Management Today*);
- best work–life balance of any UK organization (*Financial Times*);
- best for positive impact on society of any UK small business (Business in the Community);
- best for promoting staff health and well-being of any UK company (Great Place to Work Institute).

In addition Happy has been listed as one of the best 20 workplaces in the UK (in the *Financial Times*/Great Place to Work Institute annual awards) for the last five years.

In this short volume, packed with stories and practical examples, Henry sets out the simple principles that could transform your workplace into a truly great place to work in.

Outside work Henry is a parent, a governor in his local school and a very keen cyclist. In 2008 and 2010 he successfully completed the *étape du tour*, the public stage of the Tour de France.

Foreword

As a researcher and consultant, I have been trying for many years to figure out how to improve the effectiveness of our business organizations – to make them more engaging, more fulfilling and more productive. And the heart of the challenge is the following puzzle.

Everyone wants to work in an engaging, exciting workplace. We create ranking lists of the 'best places to work'. We read research that shows consistently that happier, more engaged employees are more productive. We know, intuitively, that a workplace where people come first is the workplace we want to be part of.

And yet the vast majority of workplaces are stultifyingly dull. The physical surroundings are drab. Many jobs are designed to be as repetitive and soulless as possible. Fear is endemic. Many bosses, as Stanford's Bob Sutton would say, are assholes.

Why the enormous disconnect between these two worldviews? There are plenty of partial answers to this question, but the heart of it is that most of us simply know no different. We accept the bureaucratic, hierarchical, control-ridden world we have grown up with, and we assume that it is a necessary part of our working life. The only solution – apart from simply putting up with it – is to quit and become a freelancer or an entrepreneur. Indeed, many people go down this route, and once they have stepped out of the corporate machinery very few go back.

This tacit acceptance of the status quo happens in large part because we lack good role models, examples of what a genuinely engaging workplace could look like. And this is where Happy Ltd and Henry Stewart come in.

I first met Henry five years back, interviewing him in his offices for an article I was writing. I was immediately attracted to the playful and informal ambience he had created at Happy, and by the force of his personality. Henry had experienced the bad old world of corporate bureaucracy, and he had resolved to do things differently when he started his own company. And he has succeeded. You can sense it when you walk through the doors in Happy. And you can see the evidence in the awards they have won.

Henry has put together his own unique set of management principles. Some of them are pretty obvious, some are pretty radical. But the point is that they are not just the random musings of a management thinker; rather, they are the principles on which he has built his company. He lives by them, and he has proved that they work.

Companies like Happy are more important to the economy than the immediate value they create for their customers and employees. They represent an important source of inspiration for management entrepreneurs everywhere who are looking for ideas for how to make their workplaces more exciting and fulfilling. Of course, it would be nonsense to think that another company could simply pick up Henry Stewart's principles and adopt them for themselves. They were designed for the particular set of challenges facing Happy Ltd, and there are questions about how scalable they are beyond a company of a certain size. But such caveats miss the point. The real point is that we live in a world of work where so much of it is so drab and boring that most people cannot imagine an alternative. We need fresh and exciting role models. Happy Ltd is such a model. Read the book, and heed Henry's command to 'make your organization a great workplace – now'.

Professor Julian Birkinshaw of
London Business School

Introduction

Imagine a workplace where people are energized and motivated by being in control of the work they do. Imagine they are trusted and given freedom, within clear guidelines, to decide how to achieve their results. Imagine they are able to get the life balance they want. Imagine they are valued according to the work they do, rather than the number of hours they spend at their desk.

Wouldn't you want to work there? Wouldn't it also be the place that would enable you to work at your best and most productive?

There are many great places at which to work. These are organizations where people feel trusted, where management is truly supportive; organizations that avoid the bureaucracy and levels of approval that too often get in the way of innovation. Listed at the top of the annual lists of best workplaces, these companies are proof that the work environment can be structured to help people to fulfil their potential.

But in too many organizations management is broken. In one global survey just 21 per cent of staff reported that they are fully engaged at their workplace.[1] As Professor Gary Hamel of London Business School commented, 'the other 79 per cent may be physically on the job, but they've left their enthusiasm and ingenuity at home'.

This is a huge waste and also a huge opportunity. If that level of engagement can be increased, then productivity and innovation can rocket. Not only is this possible, but it can be done at far lower cost than many of the investments that companies engage in to improve their businesses.

The Happy Manifesto is a call for change. It is a call to create better, and happier, workplaces. It is a call to look at management from the perspective of the people who are managed. It is a call to transform the way management works and focus its efforts on what is needed to make people more effective.

I learnt these lessons the hard way. My journey to this point started in a truly disastrous enterprise. In the 1980s I was involved in the project to set up a radical campaigning left-of-centre Sunday newspaper, called *News on Sunday*. We raised £6.5 million in investment. Six weeks after the launch, we had lost the lot. It was quite a learning experience.

We hired some fantastic people, talented and motivated. And then, inadvertently, we created a working environment where it was almost impossible for these highly capable individuals to succeed. Although it was set up on the basis of great ideals, we had in fact created a company that was badly managed and terrible to work in, and where nobody was able to perform at their best.

I left there determined to create a company that was both principled and effective, and a great place to work in. That company is Happy, a training business. Our Happy Computers division trains people in desktop software, making learning about computers an involving and enjoyable experience. Our Happy People division helps organizations create great workplaces based on the ideas I outline in this book. Happy is still a long way from achieving everything I would want. But, having learned from many other enterprises along the way, we have been recognized as creating a rather unique workplace.

The benefits of a great workplace are widespread. Motivated and energized employees lead to better customer satisfaction, lower staff turnover, less sick leave and easier recruitment. Which all leads to greater growth and profitability. It is not just me saying this. Later in the book, you will see examples and evidence of the clear financial benefits of treating your people well.

The Happy Manifesto sets out simple ideas and principles that can enable a change in the way people work. It is packed with real-life case studies, where we – or other organizations – have implemented these ideas and seen the benefits. The aim is both to challenge you and to give you specific ideas you can put into practice straight away in your workplace.

Note

1 Tower Perrins survey, quoted in 'The hidden costs of overbearing bosses' by Gary Hamel, *Labnotes*, Issue 14, December 2009, London Business School Mlab.

Chapter One
Enable people to work at their best

In this book I will set out what I believe are the keys to a great workplace, using examples from Happy and from many other organizations. But first I want to ask you a couple of questions, and prompt you to think about your own experience.

What makes great management?

So what makes great management? Stop for a moment and note down three or four key elements of what you need to do to be a great manager. Avoid using the words 'management' or 'leadership', as the task is to describe what these are:

....

....

The single most common response, in the United States and UK at least, is 'good communication'. This is followed by 'clear vision', 'being decisive' and 'integrity'. Others also list 'support', 'listening skills' and similar phrases. Before we examine which are the most useful answers, let's look at another angle.

When did you work at your best?

Take a moment to think about when you worked at your best. Bring to mind a real example of a time when you were really proud of what you achieved. Once you have a specific example in mind, answer these questions about it:

- Was it a time characterized by being especially well paid?
- Was it a time when communication from your manager, or the organization, was particularly strong?
- Was it when you were given a real challenge?
- Was it a time when you were trusted and given freedom to do your job your way?

I have asked these questions of thousands of people and the answers are always similar. When I ask my audiences to raise their hands in response to these questions, virtually none go up in response to pay. We all deserve to be well paid for what we do, but that is not a key element in what motivates us to work at our best.

Normally around one-quarter of the audience feel it was a time of good communication. Again, this is not the key factor. Generally over half respond that it was a time when they were challenged. But consistently, across audience after audience, the element that is involved more than any other, and crops up in the vast majority of examples of when people work at their best, is that they were trusted and given the freedom to carry out the task in their own way.

Most people accept that this is true of themselves. But it will also almost certainly be true of the people you manage. To enable them to work at their best, and to ensure they are motivated to do so, you need to find a way to put them in control of their job. That is what this book is about.

Questions: Is it true of you that your best work was when you were trusted and able to find your own way to the objective?

Do you give the people you manage the same level of trust that enabled you to work at your best – and what would be different if you did?

Trust and freedom

The two questions above are really the same question asked in different ways. What makes great management should be the same as what enables you to work at your best. If being trusted is what enabled you to work at your best, then trusting your staff should be the first thing people think of when asked what makes great management. But, in the UK or United States at least, it rarely is.

Get out of the way: less management can mean more productivity

One of my favourite management stories is that of Tom Tribone, who found himself, at the age of 24, managing a small chemical plant employing 130 people. After some time there, carrying out a traditional management role, he realized that the plant produced only 2 million pounds a month of latex goo during the working day, but doubled to a rate of 4 million at weekends. As Robert Waterman explains:

> To Tribone, this was an amazing statistic – the weekend blip. What was it about weekends? The conclusion was inescapable. The plant did better – two times better – when he wasn't around. Once he learned this, the plant began setting production records. 'The most effective direction I could give my people was simply to log the orders that came to the plant and convey that data,' Tribone says. 'These folks know how to run the plant. If they knew what the customer wanted, and didn't have too much interference from me, they got it done.'
>
> (From *Frontiers of Excellence* by Robert Waterman)

It is not that Tom had been a bad manager. He was doing his best to help, regularly walking the shop floor and seeking to help his workers and discuss with them how to improve their work. He was well-meaning but, in reality, he was just getting in the way of people who knew how to do their job well.

Getting managers out of the way

In long-gone days my colleague Cathy Busani used to work in a housing association where they had one typing pool serving all the housing officers in the organization. The typing pool had a manager and the staff would negotiate with the manager of the housing officers about workload and response times when housing officers submitted handwritten work or audio cassettes to be typed out.

The two managers met regularly, and set rules for how things should be done. But somehow it never seemed to work. Neither of the groups of staff were happy. The typists felt the officers made unreasonable demands and the housing officers felt the typists were not responsive enough.

Cathy was asked to step in at this point and persuaded the departments to try a new approach. She asked the managers to step out of the negotiation and got the typists and officers to talk directly to each other, encouraging them to find their own solution. Suddenly they were able to understand each other's needs. And without having to set absolute rules, they could explain where they could be flexible and where they found the demands unreasonable.

The result: the officers understood the typists' work and how to approach them when they did have an urgent need. The typists felt understood and appreciated. And the managers had less to worry about and more time to focus on their real job, supporting their people.

Typing pools may be a thing of the past. Younger readers may not even know what I am talking about. But this example highlights a common mistake that managers make. Many see their role as to defend their staff against unreasonable expectations from other parts of the organization, and they take a lot of pride in doing so.

There is a role for managers to support their people when faced by the demands of more senior people in the company. But – as in the typing pool example – doing it on behalf of your people prevents flexibility and often gets in the way of solutions that meet everybody's needs.

Questions: Where do you still get involved in the details of how people do their jobs?

How can you step out of the way, enabling them to decide how to do the work?

Pre-approve it

I've talked about great management being about getting out of the way. Here is a way you can put this into practice now.

Do you ever set up an individual or a group of people to solve a problem, make improvements or come up with a new product or a new way of doing things, and ask them to come back to you with a solution? How would it be if, next time you do this, you 'pre-approve it'? You make clear that you do not need to approve or check the proposal and that the group has full authority to go ahead and implement it.

Some managers find this idea scary. But think for a moment. What effect would this have on how seriously people took the task? We find it instantly removes any play-acting and politics. Suddenly, it's for real.

And what effect would it have on the likelihood that they will make it work? Well, they own the proposal. They have a much greater investment in making it work. And when something goes wrong they can't blame it on the 'improvement' that management insisted upon.

Of course the group (or individual) needs clear guidance. They need to know the budget. They need to know the key pieces of information you have locked away in your brain, which often only emerge when you explain it can't be done that way. And they need to know which people and which departments will be affected, so that they can clear it with them. Pre-approval works at all levels of the company. I remember two exit interviews one year, with two of our most junior members of staff. Both stated that the best thing about working for Happy had been that they had been trusted to come up with their own solutions and allowed to implement them without approval.

One was our receptionist. When she asked if she could make the reception area more welcoming, she was given a budget to do what she felt was needed – and, once we'd ensured she understood the culture and brand of Happy, she was pre-approved to implement the changes. The other person worked in our café and was able to implement steady changes, testing them as she went but not needing to seek approval as she tried out these new approaches. In both cases, the first time I saw the proposals was when I walked into the office and saw what had changed.

These examples, though they refer to small things, are important. If every one of your people is motivated to make the small changes that make a difference for your customers, and doesn't have to go through levels of approval to do so, you can experience genuine continual improvement.

Pre-approval has a very positive effect on a company culture. It encourages people to take more ownership and responsibility for their work. It also encourages innovation and creates a culture of looking for solutions.

Pre-approval: Happy's website

The scariest thing I pre-approved was our new website, launched in 2011. As we don't advertise nor have sales-people at Happy Ltd, most of our sales come through word-of-mouth recommendation and the website is just about our only external marketing tool. It is many people's first experience of our company and must reflect our values.

In the past the production of the website had been a bit of a mismatch. There was always a member of staff working on it but, given its importance to Happy, I always felt it necessary to be closely involved. The result was dis-satisfaction all round, with the people responsible never feeling they could truly do what they wanted.

I decided it was time to put into practice what I've been recommending, to step out of the way and pre-approve it. Jonny Reynolds, who had been with us for four years working in our customer service team and had previous experience in web development, took on the task. There were some clear parameters: there was a budget (quite a tight one); it had to reflect the Happy brand, including a clear yellow element – we had just been through a branding exercise; and there were one or two specific details, such as using sans serif fonts.

Also, I made sure that Jonny had the skills needed to do the job. We sent him on the best SEO (Search Engine Optimization) course we know of, and linked him to experts in the field of social media. We agreed what the site would be judged on and the kind of key words that we would optimize. Then, as the site developed, I resisted the temptation to look at the plans and the detailed layout. The first time I saw how the website would look was a couple of days before it launched.

Jonny did a remarkable job. Visitors to the website trebled and income generated doubled. All the feedback from employees and clients has been hugely positive. Beforehand you could rarely find us in Google unless you actually typed in 'Happy'. Now people are finding us through the things we know are important: phrases like 'Excel training London' and 'BSL signer job' (which we are recruiting for at the moment). I feel that getting out of Jonny's way has been crucial to the success of the website and that the benefits to Happy will be massive. Check it out at **www.happy.co.uk**.

Questions: Where can you, in the next few days, pre-approve an individual or group to come up with a new approach? (Feel free to start with something small.)

What do they need to know, who do they need to talk to and what resources do they need to make sure their solution will be appropriate?

Step out of approval

What was the most important thing I did to develop leadership in BP? I told people who came to me for help that I couldn't help them, they had to work it out for themselves (even if I knew the answer).

Lord Simon, Chief Executive, BP, 1992–97[1]

I received an e-mail from one of our freelance trainers, to thank me for three things we'd recently changed that made life easier for her. As I read the examples, a couple of things struck me. First, I had not been aware that these changes had been made. Second, I realized that, if they had gone across my desk for approval, I would have rejected at least two of the three proposals.

I had originally set up most of the systems for training here at Happy. These were all my ways of doing things and, like most managers, I had a natural resistance to changing the methods that I had devised. Once a proposal is on my desk it is hard to ignore it, and especially difficult to resist the temptation to 'improve' it. Be honest now: how have you felt when one of your ideas or proposals has been 'improved' by your manager?

I realized the only way to ensure I don't get in the way of perfectly good proposals, and I recommend it to you, is: make sure new ideas don't have to go across your desk for approval.

A lot of managers find this difficult. 'But I've got all this knowledge and experience,' they explain. 'Without that expert comment, they could get it wrong.' And it is true that managers often have vital information that is crucial in any change. But there are two ways of approaching that.

One is to ensure that managers have to approve proposals. The other is to spread the knowledge and make sure front-line staff are trained up with all the information they need to make good decisions.

This doesn't mean that nothing is ever checked. There is a principle at Happy that you get somebody else to check through anything external, but it doesn't have to be your manager and it isn't about approval. In fact the best proofer at Happy is probably Suzi – one of our newest, and youngest, members of staff.

Enabling your people to be trusted

Some years ago, working with a large campaign organization on making management more effective, I realized that many staff were demotivated. They did not feel trusted, and gave as an example that any external statement or press release needed several levels of approval. One employee told us he deliberately put items of nonsense into his press releases to see if his managers spotted them and removed them. After all, what went out was not his responsibility. It was the job of others to make sure it was right.

The senior management understood the problem but explained that the credibility of the organization depended on its information being absolutely accurate, consistent and seen as impartial. And the fact that they did find mistakes only reinforced the belief that the levels of approval were necessary. This left a dilemma. The need for approval was demotivating staff, removing their sense of ownership, and making them lazy about checking key facts. But if staff were able to release whatever they wanted, senior management feared it could undermine the organization.

After attending one of our 'Management is Fun' courses the managers decided to take the radical step of abolishing their approval procedures. They would explain clearly what was expected, what kind of checks they needed to make, where staff could go for advice if they were unsure of anything and who they should think about consulting. But the member of staff would have final sign-off responsibility. These steps are crucial. They did not simply let staff write whatever they wanted, but trained them in what was needed – making clear what it was that those giving the approval knew that the writer might not know.

'What was the result?' asks David Bull, who was then Director of the organization.

> There were far fewer arguments about approvals (though
> sometimes someone wasn't consulted who felt they
> should have been). We all saved an enormous amount
> of management time, which we put into supporting our
> staff. The staff felt their managers were helping instead of
> checking up. The managers could focus on the big picture,
> so goals became clearer. Morale improved, management
> really did start to be more fun – and the quality of published
> material gradually improved – and, as people gained in
> confidence, they became more innovative and creative.

David Bull has since become Executive Director of UNICEF. Talking to me now, several years later, he confirms how the change transformed the work of managers. Many had previously spent long hours checking information, effectively doing the researchers' job again. After the change they were freed up to do their key jobs, both the strategic element and the role of supporting and coaching their people.

When he moved to UNICEF, David introduced the Common Approach to Management, based on these concepts. The idea is that within clear agreed objectives and parameters, staff are trusted and given freedom and the confidence of their managers. As David explains, 'the other side of this coin is accountability. If there is success it should be celebrated and shared. If not, there should be acceptance, learning and improvement rather than blame or denial.

> In this approach it is not possible to say: 'It's not my fault – my manager should have been checking up on me.' The manager should be there to provide support, coaching and advice. The Common Approach represents a belief not only that a trusting and mutually supportive environment gets the best out of people, but also that HOW we work is important as well as what we achieve. It is concerned with being clear about, and committed to, our values, and protecting and nurturing them as we grow and change. So far we have been pretty successful too, thanks to our great people.

Questions: What knowledge do you or your managers have that, if you passed it on to your people, would enable you to step out of approval?

How can you train up your people with this information? When will you do it?

Does your structure help innovation?

When I speak at large conferences I like to ask the audience to raise their hand if they would like their organization to be more innovative. Virtually every hand goes up.

My follow-up question is a simple one. I ask them to keep their hands raised if they believe the levels of approval they have in their companies help them to be more innovative. Whatever the level of the people in the organization, whether front-line staff or senior management, there are never more than one or two hands still in the air.

This is the reality in most organizations. They call for people to come up with new ideas, new products, new ways of doing things. But then they keep in place a structure that gets in the way of these ideas taking shape and, too often, gives people a clear message that it isn't worth trying.

Seeking management approval

On one of my courses I had a group of staff from the help-line of a healthcare charity. Their job was to field calls, and to provide information on diabetes – principally to those with diabetes, but also to relatives of people with the condition.

They were highly motivated, wanted to do the best job possible and so wanted to set up feedback on how they were doing. They met and agreed a set of five questions that they would ask at the end of each call to check how the call had gone, and what they could do better next time.

> They put their proposal to management for approval. It went through various levels, and across the desks of a range of managers. Eventually, a month later, a revised and improved version came back... with *30* questions to be asked at the end of each call. This was, of course, absurd and destroyed any ownership of the proposal by the help-line staff. They never introduced the feedback and became less motivated.

This may seem an extreme example, but when I tell the story on my courses, people nod in recognition. The problem is that, if you are asked to check and approve something, it is only human nature to try to add something and improve it – whether through a need to justify your role or because you genuinely want to help. The way to stop this happening is to make sure that proposals don't need to go across other people's desks for approval.

Questions: Does your structure encourage new ideas, or inhibit them by putting barriers in their way? (Hint: ask your people what they think.)

How can you enable people with great ideas to put them into practice, with as few delays as possible?

Encourage disobedience

A new approach to e-learning

In 1999 we were trying to work out how to get involved in
e-learning. It was the midst of the first internet boom and many
people were arguing that online learning would replace the
classroom. I set Lucy Blake the task of researching the options
and coming up with a Happy approach.

My belief was that it should not involve creating our own
materials, as that would definitely be too expensive, but
instead we should build a portal that integrated other people's
materials. Indeed, part of the remit was specifically not to
create our own materials but to find the best that was out
there.

Lucy took two months, consulted widely, and came back
with a completely new approach to e-learning based on
building our own materials. She deliberately hadn't checked in
with me because she knew I might oppose the idea in the
early stages and she knew she had been tasked to find a
solution.

That solution was the basis of the work of our e-learning
division for the next eight years and was responsible for
a £1 million contract with the National Health Service and a
£500,000 contract with the Department of Work and Pensions.
Neither would have been won if my approach had been
followed.

What was vital here was that Lucy knew that, within the Happy culture, it was more important to come up with a great solution than to follow instructions. Generally I try to avoid telling people what to do but, if I do, I know there is a fair chance the member of staff will do something completely different anyway, if it seems a better way to help the customer or achieve the result that is needed.

Google's second biggest revenue earner, Adsense, stems from a similar act of disobedience. Back in 2002 their e-mail product, gmail, was still in development and two Googlers (Google staff) were working on improving it. Paul Buchheit was keen to try context-sensitive adverts but had been told by his colleague Marissa Mayer that they would never work effectively. Sergey Brin, founder of Google (with Larry Page), was known to be strongly against targeting ads based on what users were reading rather than what they were searching for. Buchheit had agreed not to try them.

Despite this clear understanding that he was not going to pursue it, Buchheit went ahead one day in 2002 and worked through the night to produce a working version of advertisements that were displayed in response to what was in the e-mails. When Brin and Page were shown the system in action the next day, they were reportedly delighted with what they saw. This determination to go against instructions led to a multi-billion-dollar income.[2]

The key issue here is the culture of your organization. Innovation rarely comes from the top. Indeed senior managers are all too often barriers to change. Often it needs one or more determined individuals who are prepared to try out new ideas, even if they are counter to what they have been told or asked to do. Sometimes they will fail.

But sometimes they will succeed brilliantly, as in these examples.

Questions: Does your culture encourage innovation to the point of disobedience?
What stories can you tell to build that kind of culture?

The myth of the clever manager – lessons from *Boss Swap*

In 2004 a television programme called *Boss Swap* was shown on Channel 4 in the UK. It was a spin-off from the far more popular *Wife Swap*. Instead of two wives swapping places, the bosses of two companies were exchanged. There were three programmes and so six bosses were involved altogether. Five of these swaps were disastrous, which is possibly the reason the programme never ran again.

The problem was that these managers clearly saw their role as to know everything, to work out what was wrong in their new companies and tell people how to improve things. This was despite the fact that they had no knowledge of the industry and were working with people who had years of experience. They marched in and started telling people what to do, with predictable results for morale and motivation.

One manager took a different approach. On arrival at the new company he walked round the shop floor, asking staff what ideas they had, what got in their way, and what they would suggest for improvements. This was the only one of the six swaps to be a success.

Many managers believe, consciously or unconsciously, that they have been chosen to manage because they are cleverer than others. A key part of their role, they assume, is to work out better ways of doing things. The result is a very stressful time for the manager.

The alternative is to focus on supporting the team and helping them to make the right decisions. The great thing about this approach is that it immediately removes a key part of the stress of being a manager.

'I used to interfere in everything,' explains Ella Heeks, who was Managing Director of organic delivery company Abel & Cole as it grew from £0.5 million sales to £20 million.

> In my case it wasn't even that I thought I knew best. I saw it as my responsibility as MD to deal with problems and not to leave people to cope on their own. Anything else I would have seen as shirking my job.
>
> I ended up working up to 80 hours a week. With the new approach I learnt from Happy, I spent time instead sitting with people, agreeing what the problem was and what was needed. And then left them to find the best solution. I got my life back, people were happier in their work and decisions were at least as good as I had been making.

I tested an interesting angle on this at a conference of a medical regulatory organization. Using electronic voting technology, I asked over 400 people what was most important in their boss, either:

It is most important for my manager to be effective;

or

It is most important for my manager to be supportive.

Obviously we'd prefer managers to be both. But, given a choice, 32 per cent thought it more important that their manager be effective, while 68 per cent thought it more important that they were supportive. As one member of the audience added: 'If they support us well enough, it doesn't matter how effective they are. We will cover for them when they get things wrong.' I suspect you would get a similar result in most organizations.

Questions: Where do you still assume it's your job to work out the best way for your people to do things?

What would life be like if you gave up on that, and saw your key role as supporting others to make decisions and come up with their own solutions?

Notes

1 As described by Nicholas Ferguson, ACEVO Chief Executive Summit, 12 June 2008.

2 From *Planet Google* by Randall Stross.

Chapter Two
Make your people feel good

The key focus for managers

One of the core beliefs that underlies everything we do at Happy is this:

People work best when they feel good about themselves.

Think about that statement. Do you agree with it? I find that the overwhelming majority of people do. Assuming you are in agreement then there is a natural follow-up question:

What then should be the key role of management in your organization?

By simple logic, if the first statement is true, the key role of management should be to create an environment where people feel good about themselves. It is that simple. I like to ask my audiences to put their hands up if they work for companies where that is the key focus. Normally one or two hands, out of an audience of 100 or more, will go up.

Yet if you look at some of the most successful companies on this planet – such as Microsoft, Google or

Gore – creating a great workplace is often one of their key strategic objectives.

Nando's – happy people are the key

Nando's is a popular restaurant chain in the UK, specializing in spicy chicken. Some years ago they undertook research to find out what were the key factors that explained why sales at some of their restaurants grew faster than at others.

After detailed analysis they found one factor stood out above all others in explaining the difference. This was how happy the staff were, as measured in the annual staff survey. As a result they changed their managers' bonuses so that 50 per cent was based solely on those staff survey results.

Nando's still wanted to maximize growth and profits, of course. However, they believed that the way to achieve that was not to target these elements but instead to target the key factor that creates growth and profits, namely how happy its staff were. They sent a clear message to their managers: 'Your key focus should be on making your staff happy.'[1]

Following up the story from Nando's, I discovered that the new bonus system had proved difficult and had been withdrawn after a year. Sadly some of the less effective managers focused more on trying to persuade their staff to give good scores than on actually changing the workplace. But Nando's belief in the connection between staff satisfaction and results continues, based on their experience and their research findings. Indeed in 2010, with 6,300 staff and 220 restaurants, Nando's was voted the best large business to work for in the UK in the *Sunday Times* annual list.

A similar story is told by David Smith, who was Head of People at the supermarket chain Asda from 1990 to 2007. At one point in 1990 Asda was just 10 days from bankruptcy. They turned it around and grew to the company they are today: £18 billion in sales, 170,000 employees and rated the Best Place to Work in the UK in 2008 (in the *Sunday Times* list). How did they do this? According to David, it was by focusing on their people.

Key principles included 'work made fun gets done' and 'hire for attitude' (more on that one later). The turnaround was based on a real focus on engaging front-line staff. Their internal measure of employee engagement went from 55 per cent in 1990 to 91 per cent in 2008.

'We have 360 separate P & Ls [Profit and Loss accounts] and I have done the calculations,' explains David. 'There is an absolute positive correlation between staff engagement and profitability. If a branch can achieve an engagement level of 94 per cent I guarantee the profits will grow exponentially.'[2]

Questions: What can you do, as a manager or a colleague, to make your people feel good now?

How would your organization be different if its key focus for management was on making its people happy?

Believe the best

Janet had been one of the most reliable front-line staff in the company. Suddenly that changed. She was often off sick or late to work. When she was there, her heart no longer seemed to be in the job. Some companies would have started disciplinary procedures or other forms of coercive management.

This company believed in assuming the best of their people. They took the time to find out why this previously well-motivated employee was now performing so badly. She was not keen to talk about it, but eventually explained that she was in financial difficulties. She had borrowed a small amount from a loan shark, just £50 for a pair of trainers for her daughter for Christmas. But the amount owing had ballooned and she was having difficulty paying it back. She was worried sick about the consequences.

Once the company discovered this, it was an easy matter to solve. They paid off the loan shark and, over time, took the money owing from the woman's salary. She was hugely grateful and returned to being a strongly motivated and reliable member of staff – indeed, she became more loyal than ever.

I would like to think that most companies would support their loyal staff in this way. However, several steps are needed. First, the company needs to start from a position of believing the best of its people. Second, it must have a good enough relationship between the member of staff and the manager to be able to cover a personal issue such as this. Finally, the company needs to be prepared to carry out this sort of remedy, and not be too restricted by its own rules.

People don't wake up and go to work wanting to do a bad job. Indeed a core belief at Happy is that every person you meet is doing the very best they can, given their background, experience and current circumstances.[3] This, of course, includes yourself.

It is easy to get annoyed and frustrated when people seem to be performing badly. Instead, try to think about the challenges in your workplace and how you would approach them if you start by believing the best of the people involved.

In the early days of Happy, when we had only three employees, a new member of staff had started and it didn't seem to be working out. I'd held a couple of difficult meetings with her and was starting to micro-manage her work, which was making things worse.

I discussed the situation with more experienced colleagues and they suggested I had to step back, give her a chance and really try to make it work. From that point the situation changed and Toni became a valuable member of staff, working hard to fulfil her tasks. At her next appraisal I asked what had caused the change. Her answer was simple: 'You started believing in me.'

Henry Ford famously said, 'Whether you believe you will succeed or believe you will fail, you are probably correct.' His point was that your expectation will determine the result. The same is true of others. I would rephrase it as follows:

Whether you believe the person you are managing will succeed or believe they will fail, you will probably be proved correct.

I think it was Richard Branson who said that you should never make rules on the basis of the 2 per cent of your workers who are disruptive or deliberately poor performers. Instead, set them for the 98 per cent who come to work every day seeking to do their best.

Management the Google way

Lara Harding is 'People Programs Specialist' at Google, which was voted the best workplace in the UK in 2008 (in the *Financial Times* awards). I asked her what they do when somebody is underperforming. 'We coach and mentor the hell out of them,' was her response.[4]

Questions: Is your first reaction to a problem with any of your people to believe the best of them and work from that belief?

Are your systems and processes based on the assumption that people are seeking to do a great job?

Believe the best of everybody you deal with

This principle can be extended to everybody you work with. My colleague Diye Wareibi, whose Digibridge company provides our technical support, gave a great example. One of his clients owed him money, and Diye described how he changed his debt-collecting strategy after borrowing a copy of *How to Win Friends and Influence People* from our bookshelf.

This classic book, written by Dale Carnegie in the 1930s, encourages you to understand the people you work with and to 'walk in their shoes'. As Diye explains:

> I had been chasing this debt for weeks, and it was getting increasingly antagonistic. I had threatened legal action and he had responded with 'see you in court'.
>
> After reading the book I took a different approach. I knew he had been having a difficult time and there had been health problems in his family. So I e-mailed him and then we talked on the phone. I expressed my concern and my understanding that he had been having a difficult time and asked if there was any way I could help.
>
> We had a really good talk and I think that meant something to him because I know others had been giving him a really hard time. I didn't mention the debt at all. But, you know what, within a few days I got a cheque for £1,000 in the post. And, just today, I got a second one paying the debt off in full. Treating him as a friend and trying to understand where he was coming from resulted in my bill getting paid. And hopefully we will continue to do business together for many years.

As I write this I have just succeeded in getting a full refund of £260 on a fine when my car was clamped and towed away. On one of our contracts we actually train people who deal with complaints about parking issues (in how to improve their service) and I know the abuse they have to put up with. When we ask delegates to give examples of a time when a customer has treated them well, they often find it hard to come up with any examples. The best they can often think of is people who haven't actually shouted at them.

I was annoyed about the car being towed and having to spend hours getting it back, especially as I felt I'd gone out of my way to park it legally (there was a very small notice stating that, for this short piece of road, parking was not allowed there on Sundays). But I knew these were people, like all of us, just trying to do a good day's work. So when I wrote I sought to make them feel good. I told them I was a big supporter of their work, as they keep London moving (which is true). And I commended their staff on being friendly and helpful (which they were), while explaining why I felt they had 'inadvertently' got it wrong in this case. The result of this pleasant, positive complaint was that – despite being legally in the wrong – I got my money back in full.

People work best and think best, and act most flexibly, when they feel good about themselves. Anything we can do to understand where they are coming from and make them feel positive will always go towards building trust and helping us get what we want. Think of your own experience: do you work best when shouted at, or when you are supported and made to feel good?

Questions: Do you always try to 'walk in their shoes' and understand other people's position?

Where could you do more in your everyday contacts to make others feel good?

Systems not rules

When Happy Computers was voted the best company in the UK for customer service,[5] I asked one of the judges why we had won it. He answered that it was clear we knew exactly what our customers wanted.

'But', he continued, 'that is not unusual. We find that most companies understand very well what their customers want. But they then put in place a set of rules and systems that make it almost impossible for their front-line staff to deliver what their customers want. You don't, you give people the freedom to solve the customers' problems.'

In many organizations the response to something going wrong is to create a new rule. Over time they end up with more rules than anybody can possibly remember, many of which are no longer relevant.

An example is our local reservoir, which has been turned into a leisure area, with canoeing, sailing and a café. It used to be the case that families would walk beside the water, their children playing around them, to enjoy this marvellous oasis of calm in the middle of urban London. Then it all changed, most of the reservoir was fenced off and everybody, apart from those participating in water-sports (and wearing a life jacket), was banned from being beside the water.

I asked why the change had happened. 'We had some people nearly drown,' explained the manager. 'There was a wedding reception and at midnight the bride and groom tore off their clothes and jumped in. They were both drunk and had to be rescued.'

For me this was a classic case of imposing restrictions on everybody that severely reduced people's enjoyment, as a result of one very specific incident. The irony is that it will stop hundreds of people happily enjoying walking alongside the water but won't protect against the one problem they had – drunken guests at midnight are just as likely as before to jump over the fence and leap into the reservoir.

A colleague gives a great example of this. He was once involved in reviewing a process in a housing department for approving allocation of new housing. The organization wanted to know why it was taking months to get people into new homes. The people doing the job assured their bosses that they were following the procedure to the letter.

My colleague followed the process through step-by-step. Halfway through he came to the surprising instruction: 'Wait six weeks before the next step'. This probably made sense at some time in the past, but nobody could explain why this was needed now. However, this was the process and it was faithfully obeyed.

The scariest example of obeying authority came in a classic psychological experiment in the 1950s. Nurses working on a hospital ward were phoned by somebody they didn't know, but who stated they were a doctor in the hospital. The 'doctor' asked the nurse to give a dose of medicine to a specific patient, a dose that was twice the safe limit.

The nurses had sufficient training to know the dangers of this dose but, despite this, 95 per cent of them went ahead with the instruction (until stopped by the experimenter). The rule they worked to was to follow the instructions of the doctor and, in the experiment, they did this even when somebody they didn't know gave them an instruction they knew to be dangerous.[6]

At Happy we don't leave people to simply find their own way in every situation. The logistics of our work can be complex. We have to make sure we have the right trainer in the right place at the right time, with the right materials. And, over the years, we have developed some good ways of ensuring that we do.

We talk about having systems rather than rules. There is a crucial difference between the two. A rule has to be obeyed. In response to a rule you are expected to suspend your judgement. A system is the best way we have found so far to do something. If any member of staff can think of a better way in the situation they are in, they are encouraged and expected to adapt the system.

For example, if they came to an instruction to wait six weeks in the middle of a process, they would be likely to ask around to find out why this rule existed. If nobody could think of a reason, they would put it aside and do what was necessary instead to provide the best and most responsive service to the client.

We worked with Abel & Cole, the award-winning organic food delivery company, over several years. Originally they had a system where drivers were given a printout each day of their deliveries and the order to make them in, created by a logistics expert. They were expected to follow the rules. But the drivers knew that many of the instructions did not make sense, they knew where the roadworks and the traffic jams were. However, changing the route involved a formal change request and the planners agreeing to make the change.

Instead Abel & Cole decided to put control in the hands of the drivers. They reprogrammed the software so the drivers could create their own routes, and let them decide what hours they worked. There were guidelines – they had a target for deliveries each day, and they must do everything they could to ensure the customer always got a delivery on the same day of the week.

Left to their own devices, drivers found quicker ways to get the deliveries done. Some got up as early as 3 am to get their work done before the traffic jams started. Others swapped customers to construct more sensible routes. Indeed, putting the drivers in control eventually led to a complete reorganization of the delivery system, so for example all deliveries to north-east London were on one day, and those to west London on another. This meant that drivers could work flexibly together and cover each other. The result: more satisfied drivers and more efficient deliveries, with greater reliability for the customer and cost savings for the company.

Questions: Do you have rules that must be obeyed or systems that enable people to use their judgement?

Do you put power in the hands of your front-line staff to change and improve the way they work?

Remove the rules

Netflix

At Netflix, the acclaimed US DVD-by-post service, they believe in minimizing rules. The company has no vacation policy, instead judging people on the work they do rather than the time they are in the office. Their policy on expenses, entertainment, gifts and travel is just five words long: 'Act in Netflix's best interests.' This is backed by guidance such as, 'Travel as you would if it were your own money.' Instead of laying down lots of rules, they trust their people and rely on their common sense. As one Netflix manager puts it:

> 'There is also no clothing policy at Netflix, but no one has come to work naked lately.'

> (Patty McCord, 2004)

At Twin Valley Homes, a housing association based in Blackburn, they used to have a very comprehensive rule book. 'It got in the way of helping our customers,' explained one member of staff. 'People used to find ways to use the rules to say "no".'

In their tenant survey at that time, the satisfaction results were desperately low, with one respondent going so far as to comment: 'You treat us like scum.' But all the rules were being followed to the letter. Then the organization went through a culture change. There were still key guidelines (especially on issues such as health and safety) but the key principle was to enable a response of 'Yes' wherever possible.

After the turnaround a tenant survey found 85 per cent were proud to live in a Twin Valley home and the organization won national awards for customer service. A crucial part of the change was from a rule-bound restrictive culture to one based on the principle of serving their clients.

In the spring of 2009 the most common challenge I received to these ideas was: 'How can you trust everybody? Just look at our MPs. We need rules to make sure people act properly.' It was the time of the UK MPs' expenses scandal, when many of our elected representatives were caught making absurd expenses claims (most famously, one for a house for the ducks in the MP's large back garden) and using taxpayers' money to pay off their mortgages.

But this was not a case of abuse of trust. The main defence that MPs gave was that they had obeyed the rules. This was an example of how having rules got in the way of good judgement. The question became not 'Is this a morally acceptable use of taxpayers' money?' but 'Does it fit within the rules?'

The actual solution to the MPs' expenses scandal was the one that brought it to light: transparency (although the complete transparency was actually the result of leaks to the *Daily Telegraph*). The best pressure to make an MP claim only appropriate expenses is not a more detailed set of rules but the knowledge that whatever they claim will be made public, and they will have to defend what they have done to the voters.

The same could work in your company. One possibility is to scrap your expenses rules and suggest people claim what they feel is appropriate (as Semco in Brazil have done) – but with the knowledge that details of expenses claims will be publicly available to everybody in the company.

Think about what in your organization enables people to work at their best and what doesn't. The obstacles are likely to be rigid rules and procedures, levels of approval and micro-management in general. Moving from that kind of culture to one of believing the best of everyone and making your people feel valued can transform an organization.

Making such a change may seem a daunting task. But we have helped many organizations on that journey and can testify from experience that it is achievable. Indeed, providing there is commitment from all those involved (especially senior management), it can be remarkably easy.

Questions: Does your organization have rules that get in the way of serving the customer?

What can you do to move to a workplace that enables 'Yes' wherever possible?

The key to effective change: enable, don't dictate

Resistance to change is common in organizations and I am often asked how to get over it. My first response is to ask people whether they genuinely want to facilitate whatever change is needed or whether they have a specific solution they want to put in place. The point is that the most resist-ant staff will welcome change that they have been involved in creating. People resist being changed, but not necessarily change itself.

Imagine you are not a manager. How would you get something done, involving other people, if you had no authority?

I have a friend called Marion Janner, who is a bundle of energy, always full of wacky and off-the-wall ideas. She decided she wanted to change the provision of in-hospital mental health care in the UK. It was not a modest target. It was not made easier by the fact that she held no position of authority within the mental health system. In fact her only experience, and the thing that motivated her desire for change, was as a mental health patient.

Marion couldn't tell anybody what to do. She couldn't set targets or dictate policy. But she did have lots of great ideas and a lot of imagination. So she put these together and produced the original 'Star Wards' brochure, a set of 75 ideas to put into practice on any mental health ward. These range from patients starting to manage their own medication to having pets on the ward. A recent newsletter reported a ward arranging design competitions and space-hopper races with their 'service users'.

By 18 months after its launch, over half the mental health wards in the country were taking part in Star Wards. What staff, patients, managers, commissioners and regulators have found so heartening is the speed with which small changes are being introduced, and the way these are having a substantial impact on patients' experiences. And on staff morale. This creates a virtuous cycle of motivation, energy and creativity.

Marion has been praised in a *Guardian* editorial and was one of three finalists in the *Daily Telegraph* Great Briton awards (Public Life and Campaigning category). In the 2010 New Year's Honours List, Marion was awarded an OBE for her work in improving mental health provision. All this because one person, with no ostensible power, had an idea that things could be better.

Contrast this with how the government, or conventional management, would have approached such a change. They would have started by criticizing the work currently being done (as the previous government did with teachers, police and others), and talking about the number of staff not doing a proper job. They would then prescribe a specific set of actions every ward must follow, set targets, introduce league tables, and name and shame those not doing well. Then they would wonder why the changes were not being eagerly embraced and complain that people were resistant to change.

Marion did not prescribe, she suggested. Reading Marion's newsletters you find examples only of the great work certain wards are doing. There is total respect for the professionals involved. There is no set way of doing it, just a range of ideas to try out, with people encouraged to come up with new approaches. The 'Star Wards II' publication went on to describe the many great examples of work going on.

There is another aspect to Marion's story, and that is about building alliances. Trying to work out how to get started, she visited the website of Louis Appleby, the government's National Director for Mental Health in England (known as the 'mental health tsar'). It included an invitation to get in touch if you had ideas. Marion didn't hesitate, e-mailed Louis her ideas and got a response. She followed up, met with him and – with huge energy and a clear agenda to improve the health of wards – won him over.

He introduced Marion to Malcolm Raw, a colleague with exceptional relationships in the psychiatric hospital sector. Malcolm recruited the first seven mental health wards to the scheme – the wards most likely to be early adopters of new ideas – and it spread from there. 'Chutzpah,' explains Marion. 'That's the other bit you need. Huge amounts of chutzpah.'[7]

Marion cites Happy as a key influence in getting started. 'I got from Happy this crazy idea of not telling people what to do. We provided ideas and good examples but there was no enforced action,' continues Marion. 'This idea that, if you trusted staff and worked to make them feel good, they would come up with great ways of doing things. And, amazingly, it has worked. Without you we'd probably have become a rigid standards-based project and closed within two years.'

Our belief at Happy is that people work best when they feel good about themselves. Marion's work is a living embodiment of that, and shows the effect of praise, support and encouragement. It shows what can be achieved when you rely on the innovation of well-motivated people, rather than telling people what to do. She told me it was fine to mention that she still struggles with her mental health, but that: 'Being understood and appreciated works rather better for my sanity than being judged and scolded!'

Marion achieved all this with no position of authority at all. This is an immensely useful lesson. Forget for a moment your own position. Think about what you would need to do to achieve the change you want if you didn't have that authority. As Marion puts it, try aiming for 'credibility and likeability' rather than 'authority and accountability'.

Questions: Are you seeking to impose the change you want or actively engaging your people in the change?

How would you motivate them to want to do it themselves, if you had no authority over them?

Choose less stress as a manager

I first came across these ideas when I read the book that changed my life, which in my (entirely biased) opinion is the best business book ever written: *Maverick* by Ricardo Semler. I have given away over 500 copies and every new member of staff at Happy reads it. I strongly recommend it.

Semler tells the story of how he took over Semco, a traditional Brazilian manufacturing company, from his father. He found a company where the level of trust was so low that workers were searched daily at the gates, to make sure they weren't stealing anything. After a long journey of change, the company got to the point where workers were setting their own targets, organizing their own work and – in many cases – setting their own salary. The result is that Semco has grown through several Brazilian economic crises and become one of the most popular companies to work for in Brazil.

Before I read *Maverick*, I was a fairly typical small business owner. Back then, in 1992, Happy Computers only employed three people. Despite this I was often stressed and, when on holiday, I used to ring back every day to check everything was okay. In *Maverick* I found a completely different approach. It inspired me to step back and give people space and freedom to grow.

The effect of this new approach became most clear a year later when I was ill with pneumonia and was completely out of touch for a month. I returned to find just two calls to make (this was before the days of e-mail). Everything else had been dealt with and sales had gone up.

It was a very useful lesson in how much less essential you can be than you sometimes think.

Happy has grown a lot since those early days. But that is the beauty of this approach to management. It makes life for the manager less stressful. No longer do you have to feel that all the responsibility lies on your shoulders.

What do managers do?
Coach and support

Following *Maverick* (or my interpretation of it) I had got out of the way and left people to find their own way. For some this worked very well. I remember our first trainer, Ian, absolutely thrived on it. But many people need more support. They need somebody to turn to, to help them evaluate their work and to give them attention.

As Happy grew, we put in place departmental managers, initially one for trainers and one for 'smoothies' ('smoothies' was the name chosen by our administration staff after dancing to Sade's 'Smooth Operator' one night and deciding 'Smooth Operators' was exactly how they saw themselves). The managers were elected by the staff in each department, which seemed to work well.

After a few months I noticed that our people were meeting very regularly with their managers. Most met fortnightly, some even met weekly. I was worried. I had given managers some freedom to manage in their own way, but wasn't our approach about getting managers out of the way and leaving people to it?

But it did seem to be working. People were more motivated and were certainly productive. What I realized, as I delved into what was happening, was that the training manager (Cathy Busani) had set up a system where people got a regular coaching session. This is what the best managers do. Instead of being 'managed' in any traditional sense, people were getting a space in which they were supported and encouraged to think of new approaches.

Questions: Do your people receive management or coaching from those who manage them?

Are your managers skilled in coaching and supporting their people?

Notes

1 Explained by Nando's HR specialist Marcelo Borges in a presentation to the Learning & Skills Council, 2006.

2 Presentation to London Business School Mlab Employee Engagement Seminar, October 2009.

3 This was first stated so clearly by Harvey Jackins and is encapsulated in the philosophy of Re-Evaluation Counselling. See www.rc.org.

4 Presentation at *Financial Times* Best Workplaces awards 2008.

5 *Management Today*/Service Excellence awards 2003. These awards have now been renamed the Customer Experience awards, and Happy has been a finalist for the last two years.

6 CK Hofling *et al*, 'An Experimental Study of
Nurse-Physician Relationships', *Journal of Nervous
and Mental Disease*, 143 (1966), pp 171–80. Quoted in
Influence by Robert B Cialdini.

7 Chutzpah: Yiddish term for courage bordering on
arrogance, roughly equivalent to 'nerve'.

Chapter Three
Creating a great workplace makes good business sense

The research has been done and the evidence is in. There is a clear link, shown in many studies: companies that are great workplaces are more successful commercially.

The *Financial Times*, for instance, published research into the performance of companies that appear in the 'best workplaces' lists over time. An investment in April 2001 of £100 in the 23 publicly quoted companies in the 2006 UK Best Workplace rankings would have been worth £166 by 2006, compared with £132 if the amount had been invested in the FTSE All Share Cumulative or £125 if invested in the FTSE 100.[1]

A Gallup study in 2006 of 89 organizations found that earnings per share (EPS) growth of organizations with engagement scores in the top 25 per cent was 2.6 times that of organizations with below-average engagement scores.[2]

Gallup's research has identified 12 core elements of employee engagement that they believe predict performance.

These range from knowing what is expected of you to having the opportunity every day to do what you do best, from having a supervisor who seems to care about you to staff feeling their opinions count.

Examples like these are quoted in the 2009 MacLeod report to the UK government, 'Engaging for Success', which found a wide range of evidence indicating a direct link between employee engagement and business results.[3] The report defined an engaged employee as one who 'experiences a blend of job satisfaction, organizational commitment, job involvement and feelings of empowerment'.

One example quoted by MacLeod was a global report from HR consultancy Tower Perrins in 2006, based on surveys of over 600,000 staff in a wide range of industries. 'Companies with high levels of employee engagement improved 19.2 per cent in operating income while companies with low levels of employee engagement declined 32.7 per cent over the study period.'

One of the strongest correlations was in the area of innovation. 'Fifty-nine per cent of engaged employees say that their job brings out their most creative ideas against only 3 per cent of disengaged employees.'

Of course it could be the case that a strongly performing company leads to strong engagement, rather than vice versa. Marcus Buckingham, previously of Gallup and now behind the 'StrengthsFinder' approach, 'concludes from various longitudinal studies that it is engagement that leads to performance, and this is a four times stronger relationship than performance leading to engagement' (MacLeod report, 2009).

A wide range of surveys have identified clear benefits from engaged staff:

- 70 per cent of engaged employees indicate they have a good understanding of how to meet customer needs; only 17 per cent of non-engaged employees say the same (The Chartered Institute of Personnel and Development (CIPD), 2006).[4]

- Engaged employees are 87 per cent less likely to leave the organization than the disengaged (Corporate Leadership Council, 2004).[5]

- 78 per cent of engaged employees would recommend their company's products or services, against 13 per cent of the disengaged (Gallup, 2003).[6]

These are only some of the many pieces of research that could be quoted. Again and again it has been shown that companies that engage their staff are more successful – whether measured in customer satisfaction, innovation or solid profitability and growth in share value.

Return to Abraham Maslow and the 'hierarchy of needs'

Let's return for a moment to the two questions I asked at the beginning of the book. The elements that people generally list, when asked what makes great management, are important. For people to work well, it is very useful to be clear on the organization's vision and have strong communication about what is going on. These are necessary elements, but they are not sufficient to create a great workplace. To put this in context let's remember the 'hierarchy of needs' that Abraham Maslow laid out in the 1940s.[7]

FIGURE 3.1 Maslow's hierarchy of needs

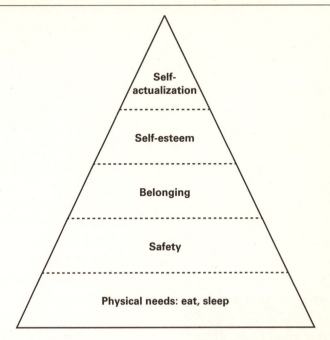

He explained that, when people don't have sufficient resources, they are driven by basic physical needs. They will be motivated by being able to eat and sleep, and then by having somewhere to live, by family and by basic health. Those elements are important and you should ensure they are being met.

When Roy Wisher started as Chief Fire Officer for Hertfordshire he asked the firefighters what got in the way of their doing a good job. He was told that their boots didn't fit, their helmets gave them headaches and the amount they got paid was often wrong. The first thing he did was to get these problems fixed. Once he'd done that he could move on to a higher level of needs.[8]

These are the basic requirements that are necessary to do the job. But they are not sufficient on their own to motivate people to reach their full potential – though they can be major obstacles if they are not in place. Beyond that come belonging and self-esteem and, above all, what Maslow called 'self-actualization'. This highest need is about personal growth and having control over one's destiny. Once people have their basic needs met, their motivation is not driven by having more to eat or more security. Instead it is these higher needs that can drive us to fulfil our potential.

If you can get in touch with people's higher motivations, then what they can achieve is normally way beyond what they can be incentivized or managed to achieve.

Learning to swim the self-actualized way

I often ask people to think of one peak achievement, one time they are really proud of. Sally gave the example of learning to swim. That might not seem a huge feat, but it was how she did it that made it so memorable. Sally never learnt to swim as a child and was 25 when she decided it was time to learn. She decided to go on a sailing holiday with friends, in the Mediterranean. She got all her friends to get in the water in a big circle, way out of her depth. And then she jumped in. And started to swim.

I like this story because it shows what people are prepared to do under their own motivation, when they are truly self-actualized. If you were managing somebody to learn to swim, you would probably set targets. You would get them to arrange lessons and, step by step, learn to swim. You would rarely tell them, 'Go and jump in at the deep end.' And even if you did, it probably wouldn't succeed – because it was your idea, not theirs and they wouldn't have the commitment to make it work.

(But don't try this at home... unless you have those very good friends around.)

Questions: First, are your people's basic needs being met? Have you asked them what gets in the way of doing their job well?

Second, what are you doing to engage people's higher motivations? Do they have the freedom and support to become 'self-actualized'?

A hierarchy of management needs

Borrowing from Maslow, overleaf I propose a hierarchy of management needs. At the bottom are communication and reward, workplace safety and comfort. These are necessary requirements to be able to work well, but they are not sufficient.

As with the Hertfordshire Fire Service example, setting your organization on the path to being a great workplace can start by getting the elements at the bottom right. If your building site is dangerous, or your furniture gives your people backache, or if people have no idea where the company is headed, it will be hard to get to the higher levels until these are sorted.

When Michael Abrashoff took over command of the USS *Benfold* for the US Navy, the first thing he did was talk to the crew about what was going well, what wasn't and

FIGURE 3.2 My interpretation: a management hierarchy of needs

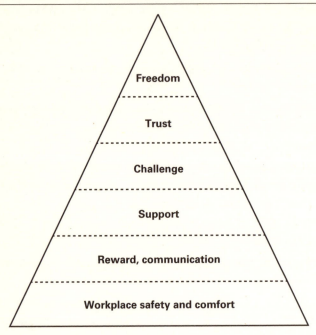

what needed to be done. He discovered that the most hated part of the job was that, when they were in dry dock, the crew members had to laboriously scrape the rust off the nuts on the bottom of the ship.

So Abrashoff did some research and discovered that the nuts could be replaced with non-rusting metal alloy for a total cost of around $40,000. It saved time and money – and just imagine the boost to motivation from not having to do that job any more. The solution seems obvious but no previous captain had bothered to listen to their staff, find out what they hated doing and get it fixed.[9]

Higher levels of management needs include support and challenge. But at the top are trust and freedom, the elements that nearly always characterize times when people work at their best. And these, of course, are closely tied to Maslow's hierarchy. It is when you have trust and freedom that it becomes possible to be self-actualized – to be in charge of and create your own destiny.

Now think about which end of the pyramid the organization you work for, or one you've worked for in the past, focuses on. Most focus on the bottom, as is clear from most people's response to the question of what makes great management. The very best companies to work for, in contrast, make sure the elements at the bottom are sorted and then focus on those at the top.

That is what this book is about. Its aim is to help you, throughout your organization, to put in place the structure to make that freedom and trust possible.

Questions: *Where is management in your organization focused at the moment?*

What would be different if the key focus was on how to challenge people, and give them the trust and freedom to work out their own solutions?

Notes

1 *Financial Times*, 18 May 2006.

2 'Return on investment in engaging employees', *Gallup Management Journal*, undated.

3 'Engaging for Success: enhancing performance through employee engagement', David MacLeod and Nita Clarke, 2009.

4 'Measuring true employee engagement', *Right Management*, 2006, CIPD.

5 'Driving performance and retention through employee engagement: A quantitative analysis of effective engagement strategies', Corporate Leadership Council 2004 (quoted in MacLeod report).

6 'Engaging for Success: enhancing performance through employee engagement', David MacLeod and Nita Clarke, 2009.

7 First published in Maslow's 1943 paper 'A Theory of Human Motivation'.

8 From the Servant Leadership conference, 2009.

9 *It's Your Ship*, Captain D Michael Abrashoff.

Chapter Four
Freedom within clear guidelines

Lessons from Tiger Woods

In 2009 *Fortune* magazine asked Tiger Woods, among others, for the 'best advice I ever got'.[1]

> When I was young, maybe six or seven years old, I'd play on the Navy golf course with my pop. My dad would say, 'Okay, where do you want to hit the ball?' I'd pick a spot and say I want to hit it there. He'd shrug and say, 'Fine, then figure out how to do it.' He didn't position my arm, adjust my feet, or change my thinking. He just said go ahead and hit the darn ball.

I think there is something profound here about how to help a talented individual develop. Let's translate it into management speak:

> When you sit down with one of your people to plan their development, get them to set their own objective. Then ask them to figure out how to achieve it. Don't tell them how to do it, let them work out their own way – with your support.

Principles and targets

A friend of mine was once given a three-word job description. His instructions were simply to 'Do cool stuff'. As you might guess, it was an internet company. I'm sure my friend Bill responded by doing some great work, but this would not work for all of us. Most organizations like to have more assurance that people will work to fulfil the organization's needs.

And most people themselves do indeed want some guidance. At one recent conference, I gave three options to a mixed group of hundreds of people. Which would they prefer?

- Complete freedom: 7 per cent.
- Freedom within clear guidelines: 89 per cent.
- Be told what to do: 4 per cent.

This is backed up by the staff surveys we carry out for clients. People rarely ask to be given free rein. Instead the most common comment is: 'Give us clear guidelines and then give us freedom to work within them.'

The Happy story

I started as an IT trainer in the late 1980s, working from my back room in Hackney, London. I was very sure of myself and believed that all I needed to be a big success, as my company grew, was to ensure everybody we employed trained as well as I did. Humility was not one of my strengths then. So, as I took on freelance trainers, I would sit in on their sessions and make detailed notes on what they did right and what they did wrong.

At the end of the day I would sit down with the trainer and feed this all back, in great detail. And how do you think this went down? Yes, like a lead balloon. The trainers somehow did not appreciate how helpful I was being!

In fact I was falling into two common management traps.

First, I was trying to get my staff to do tasks exactly the same way I did them. I was trying to create clones of myself, as many managers do. And you can only ever create a second-best clone when the best they can be is as good as you.

Second, I was trying to turn the job of training into a process. This may work in manufacturing but it doesn't work where you are serving people, because everybody is different.

But I did not want to let trainers do whatever they wanted. At the time, the standard approach in teaching people how to use computers was to put a technical person at the front of the class and have them tell people what to do. Our customers came to Happy Computers because we weren't like that. We involved people by asking questions throughout the training session, encouraged them to work things out themselves, and generally aimed to make learning about IT an enjoyable experience.

So I sat down with our small team and worked out a framework. We set down the principles within which Happy Computers trainers had to work. I remember there was a four-page guidance document, though the most important point was simple: 'Don't tell when you can ask.' This is a core principle at Happy, for training, for management and for how we work generally.

It can be as simple as asking 'Which button on the toolbar looks like it applies bullets?' instead of 'Click on the button with three dots on it to apply bullets.' Or there can be deeper questions about how they will apply this feature in their work.

And we agreed the targets they had to achieve, which were fairly clear: the learners should enjoy the day and leave confident and capable in using the software. At the time, we measured this using end-of-day evaluations; nowadays we carry out post-course surveys to evaluate the actual effect of the training on somebody's work.

This is a framework that can apply to many, if not most, jobs. If your people are working within the principles and achieving the targets, you don't need to worry about the detail. The point is to create a framework where there is freedom and flexibility, where people can innovate and come up with new approaches.

And we achieved that. Now, 20 years on, what our trainers have been able to achieve, working within the framework but coming up with new approaches, is way beyond anything I could have done. One proof of this is that eight of our trainers have been medal winners in the annual Institute of IT Training awards (with four winning Gold,[2] rating them the best IT trainer in the UK for that year), a record not matched by any other IT training company in the UK.

Questions: *What principles would you need to set down to create a framework within which people have freedom to find their own way of working?*

Are you clear, and are your people clear, on what the key targets are in each job?

Job ownership

We have brought these lessons together in what we call the Job Ownership Model. The idea is to give people the freedom to do a great job, and to give them the motivation they need within clearly agreed principles and targets. Crucial to the model is that they have the support they need and also good feedback on how well they are doing.

FIGURE 4.1   Responsibility for principles and targets

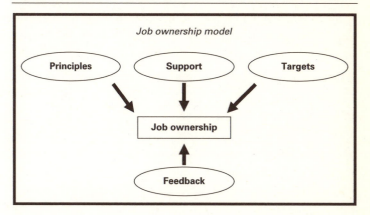

However much people are involved in their company, I would argue that the principles should be set by the company. If you get a job at Amnesty International, for example, it is no good saying that you think the death penalty is a good thing, and could you have a debate about it. Most companies have principles that are clearly laid down and are long term, and that those who join the company need to accept. In taking a job at Amnesty you are accepting these principles. The same is true of most organizations.

But who should set targets? The most common response I get is that they should be set jointly by the manager and the member of staff. To that I would respond with two questions:

- According to research, who sets the tougher targets: the manager or the member of staff?

- When is the target more likely to be achieved, when the manager sets it or when the member of staff does?

The answer to the first question is that the member of staff generally sets the tougher targets. The answer to the second is clear: a target is much more likely to have people's commitment, and be achieved, if they set it themselves.

When a new person starts with Happy, we will set their targets with them. A key element of their probationary period is to make them aware of the very high expectations we have and of the level of quality required to work here. A trainer will have a target of a score on evaluations of 92 per cent on standard measures and will know that 90 per cent is the minimum to stay working at Happy.[3]

Our expectations are high. Our core company, Happy Computers, is the only training provider in the UK to be shortlisted for IT Training Company of the Year every year for more than a decade. We have won Gold twice, Silver four times and Bronze three times. Every industry-wide survey in which Happy Computers has been included has found our customer satisfaction to be the highest in the industry.

So this is not about letting people do whatever they want. Nor is it about them defining new areas to work in. They will have some flexibility about where they focus their work, but the core targets will be set by the company's needs. But, after their probationary period, we do ask our people to decide the level of their targets – what per cent on evaluations, how much income generated, how much they will learn and develop.

This is not an easy option, but one of responsibility and accountability. Terri Kelly, Chief Executive at WL Gore, put it well in her *Wall Street Journal* interview:

> We believe that rather than having a boss or leader tell
> people what to do it's more powerful to have each person
> decide what they want to work on and where they can
> make the greatest contribution. But once you've made your
> commitment as an associate, there's an expectation that
> you'll deliver. So there are two sides to the coin: freedom to
> decide and a commitment to deliver on your promises.[4]

At WL Gore it may be the case that associates have more flexibility in what they do than we can provide at Happy. However, what we do share is a belief in delivery and accountability. All the trust that I have described, all the freedom within clear guidelines, works if there is full accountability for the results. That is the tough element.

Craig Ashby, Group Managing Director of Ardent Office Solutions in Gloucester, describes how he got a trainer to work with his salespeople to set their own targets. 'The result was that every single one set targets higher than my benchmark target.'

Questions: *Are your people clear on their targets and fully accountable for delivery?*

What can you do to increase accountability in your organization?

Support

Imagine your manager sends you a message at the beginning of the day, saying, 'I need to see you. Can you come round at 2.30 pm?' Do you feel excited? Do you spend the day looking forward to it?

To be honest, it is unlikely that you do. It would be more common for you to spend the morning worrying about that meeting. But if the focus of management is support, then a chance to meet one-to-one with your manager – to have their undivided attention – should indeed be something to look forward to.

When I outline this framework I often ask if the support indicated on the Job Ownership diagram is the same as management. Most people say no – though it could be argued that support is the same as good management. But support is something that people seek when they need it. Its frequency and its nature is determined by them. With management, it is normally the other way round. Indeed if the individual is in control of who they should ask for support, it may well not be the manager at all but whichever colleague is appropriate at that time.

Questions: *Is your management based around supporting people?*

How can you ensure your people have the support they need to do a great job?

Feedback

Feedback is a crucial part of this framework. People cannot have full job ownership if they do not know how they are doing. When I ask people how often they receive feed-back in their job the most common answer I receive is 'once a year'. Most people only get to find out how they are doing in their annual appraisal.

Let me use a football analogy here. Imagine footballers received feedback in the same way most people do in their job. Imagine they played a game and only six months later found out if they scored a goal. Or even worse, not if they scored but whether their manager thought they scored. How effective would they be as players? How easy would they find it to improve?

Feedback is a key part of the model. People need to know how they are doing and, for real job ownership, they need to be able to get this feedback outside the management structure. Your manager telling you how they think you are doing is rarely a match for customers (whether internal or external) giving direct feedback on how they think you have done.

Feedback leading to change at Rackspace

Rackspace is a web hosting company dedicated to 'fanatical support'. They won the UK Service Excellence award two years after Happy and regularly appear in the lists of the best UK workplaces. Their commitment to creating a great place to work is combined with the highest expectations of their staff. Their use of feedback includes a quarterly peer review, where each member of staff ranks their colleagues.

The first time they did this one support guy, who we shall call Jeff, came clearly bottom. Those who do badly receive a further feedback session and it was explained that his colleagues resented him because he never answered the phone – despite it being clearly part of his job. He was devastated by the results but at least he had clear information on what he needed to do. The next quarter he topped the list. Colleagues reported that they could never get to the phone because Jeff was always determined to be the first to answer it!

Ideally this feedback should be direct to the individual. The moment it is 'interpreted' by management, it is no longer owned by the member of staff. Ownership of the figures is crucial. As our training manager, Nicky Stone, comments: 'Co-ordinator meetings are so much nicer and more productive for both when it is the trainer – not me as their manager – who brings the feedback to discuss.'

We are lucky as a training company, in that every trainer receives direct structured feedback at the end of each day. For most this is seen as a positive, and the challenge in the rest of the company has been to give people as good feedback in their admin or techie roles. So we now have upward appraisals for our co-ordinators and management, peer appraisals for all staff and specific feedback for roles such as IT support and operations.

Questions: *How much feedback do your people get in their jobs?*

How can you set up more and deeper feedback, from both clients and colleagues?

It's good to keep score – providing your people are in control

Bristol City Council had a small unit within its Housing Department responsible for taking legal action against tenants who owed rent. It had a large caseload of pending work and a poor reputation for delivery. The manager, Chris Knight, had tried all sorts of methods for dealing with the backlog, based around telling people what needed to be done.

Then he decided on a different approach. Chris asked the team what would be a reasonable amount of time to prepare each case and issue the legal papers, and they said it should take no more than 10 working days.

He then set up a standard query, which would calculate the total number of days that cases were over this 10-day target. He was careful not to produce the report himself, but asked the team to take it in turns to produce the figures. That is all he asked, that they produce the figures daily and plot them on a graph on the wall beside their desks.

The first day, the figure was close to 8,000 days. But a few days later it had fallen to less than 4,000. His team had achieved this by closing off a whole set of cases that had actually been dealt with, but had not been recorded on the computer – a task the manager had been trying to get them to do for months.

Producing the figure each day, they felt a sense of owner-ship over it, and began suggesting and implementing ways to get it to fall further, including some that they had pre-viously dismissed as unworkable when the manager had proposed them. One day the manager noticed a member of staff producing the figure at the end of the day. This person normally left at 5 pm precisely, but this time when she found that the graph had not fallen, she took off her coat and said, 'Maybe I can get a few more done.' She stayed another half-hour, ran the figure again and left feeling very satisfied.

By the time Chris left the department nine months later, the figure was down below 100. His people had done all the work, including working out how to solve the issues. All he had done was help them to focus on the key figure in a way that gave them ownership.

Think carefully about this. As Chris explains:

> What was crucial to success in this case was that I asked them to say what was a reasonable time to process cases – I didn't set them a target. When they then saw how far over their own 'target' they were, they were horrified and immediately wanted to do something to deal with this crisis, one they had not previously realized even existed. If I had set the target the psychology wouldn't have been right and it wouldn't have had the same effect. The data would have been the same but the effect would have been different. Plotting that graph was also crucial. If you don't know how well you're doing, how do you know what to do next?

Chris asked me to say that he attributes his success to what he learnt from Ian Robson and his company, Perception Dynamics.[5] He found their advice crucial in ensuring the psychology was just right in this process.

Questions: Are your people clear as to what are the most important things for them to achieve?

How can they keep track of their progress in a way that gives them ownership?

Notes

1 *Fortune* magazine, 6 July 2009.

2 The four Gold winners are Cathy Busani, Donna Wheeler, Ed Lepre and Nadya Nathan.

3 Based on scoring Excellent as 5, Good as 4, Average as 3, etc.

4 'A revolutionary at work at WL Gore', *Wall Street Journal*, 23 March 2010.

5 www.perceptiondynamics.info.

Chapter Five
Be open and transparent

'Without information you cannot take responsibility. With information you cannot avoid responsibility.'

JAN CARLZON, CEO, SAS AIRLINES (1981–94)

Many years ago I worked as a researcher on a late-night television show called *After Dark*. The programme consisted of sitting seven carefully chosen people in comfortable armchairs and getting them to discuss a subject, live on air, for around three hours. Getting the right mix of people was crucial.

We were often trying to bring in guests from abroad but one oddity about the way the process was managed was that the travel budget was secret, known only to the chief executive and the production manager. As researchers we didn't know the budget, so we always took the side of the guests and sought the best possible deal for them. A real triumph was to get a Concorde flight for a guest coming from the United States.

If we had known the budget, we would have had to take responsibility and balance the needs of the guest and the company, working together to ensure that overall we met the budget. For me this was a classic example of Jan Carlzon's quote in practice – without information we couldn't take responsibility. In contrast, see below for how Happy staff took real responsibility when they were given the full facts.

At Happy all information is open, with the exception of any personal or disciplinary matters. All staff have read-only access to the whole IT network, including all financial information, except for that one folder on personal information.

This is especially true of financial information. At staff meetings, on a regular basis, I present the financial information. I use toy Duplo bricks (the larger version of Lego) to explain how sales, overheads, cost of sales and profits interact. The aim is that all staff understand the key financial dynamics of the company and the role they play in creating that profit.

The result is that all staff are well informed and very conscious of the effects of what they do. Given full information, I find they do indeed take responsibility and are very cost-conscious. Even though the company is fairly traditionally owned, our people often talk about a sense of ownership because of this involvement.

Questions: Are your people fully informed about what is going on in the company, including the finances?

What would happen if you erred on the side of providing as much information as possible?

People need bad news too

In 1996 Happy Computers was growing fast. In fact sales increased by 50 per cent in just six months. The pace of change was hectic. For a few months, it is embarrassing to remember, we didn't produce monthly management accounts. We were clearly doing well, so the exact figures didn't seem so important.

It was a near-fatal mistake. When I brought the accounts up to date I discovered that our cost-of-sales had risen so alarmingly that we had been making losses and – if we continued on the same lines – we would be bankrupt within weeks. When I reported back at the weekly staff meeting, it was one of the most difficult sessions I had ever run. All our staff had been working hard to keep up with demand and had no idea that things were going badly.

But that meeting was a turning point. Everybody got involved in finding ways to save money. In the weeks afterwards it was virtually impossible to propose spending without somebody suggesting a way to do it more cheaply. Within weeks we were back in profit and the systems we put in place to stop it happening again laid the basis of our growth over the next decade.

It is easy to keep people informed when things are going well. But it is crucially important to let people know when things are going badly.

Another example is our e-learning division, which produces interactive materials to enable people to learn online. This had become the most profitable part of our business on the basis of two large fixed-term contracts (one covering the entire National Health Service and involving 200,000 learners). Both contracts were coming to an end.

We worked together to try to create replacement income but didn't achieve it. With our income set to fall by 80 per cent, business people I knew advised me to make staff redundant or to close the department entirely. Instead we were clear with people, we explained we couldn't maintain the level of staffing and encouraged them to be open about any plans to move.

One member of staff took redundancy, because he really wanted to be a scriptwriter for UK TV shows such as *Dr Who*, *Spooks* and *Torchwood* (in which he has been successful). Over several months most of the rest of the team applied for and found other work.

The result is that we were left with the two most experienced e-learning developers, we still have a full e-learning capability (and now work more with external associates than with permanent staff), and this part of the company is profitable. Last summer we renewed our biggest government contract, for a combination of classroom and online training, something we could not have done if we had chosen to close this capability.

The individuals concerned, both those who have stayed and those who have left, feel supported by Happy and we have given a clear message that, even in difficult times, we will seek a way that helps our people rather than moving straight to what seems to be the best financial solution.

Questions: Are you open about your company's performance, even when things are not going well?

What would happen if you assumed all information should be available, unless there is a clear reason why not?

Make salaries open

At Happy what everybody earns is public knowledge within the company. Every member of staff has access to a spreadsheet that gives not only the current salary but every salary that each person has earned since they first joined the company. And, yes, that does include my salary.

Many people find that surprising and assume that, however open your organization is, salaries are one thing that must be kept secret. Why is that?

I was asked to talk about our open salaries policy on a radio programme on BBC Radio 4. As I talked to the producer before the programme, she recounted her own experience. She had found that a colleague doing the same job earned £10,000 more than she did. She confronted her boss and asked, why the difference? 'Because he asked for it and you didn't,' came the surprisingly honest answer.

When salaries are secret it is easy for rises to be based on arbitrary factors such as whether somebody asked or not. Or they can be given because somebody works later at the office, whether or not they are more productive as a result. When salaries are open there is the simple check that everybody can see the results and challenge them. It certainly focuses the mind when you are awarding a pay increase.

And even if salaries are fair, people will often assume they are not fair if they are kept secret. They will imagine that people have got rises because they stay late (even if they don't produce any more), go to the pub with their manager or are simply somebody's favourite. This is not good for morale and, sadly, without transparency, those rumours are often true.

I can't claim that everybody at Happy is satisfied with the salary they earn. But the one element that is uncontroversial is the open salaries policy. In our most recent survey, 94 per cent of those who expressed a preference said they approved of it and the majority said it helped them to understand what they could earn in the future.

In some countries this is not controversial at all. When I spoke in Norway, the idea of open salaries did not get a reaction. The reason was simple: in Norway what everybody earns is publicly available. On the internet, you can look up the tax returns for anybody you like, from your next-door neighbour to the prime minister.

Piscines Ideales

One thing I find interesting about the concept of open salaries is that, at first, people normally assume the concept is impossible, but when they consider it, they find it makes sense.

At the *Financial Times* Best Workplaces awards in Berlin in 2006 I met Stelios Stavrides from Piscines Ideales, a Greek swimming pool company, who had come in the top 10 best workplaces in Europe. We were discussing transparency and he commented that everything in his company was open. 'Except salaries, of course.'

I love to rise to a challenge like that and, as with most people, he found it hard to find a reason why they had to be secret.

At the same event two years later I met his son, who was also involved in running the business. I asked him if his father had mentioned anything about our conversation. 'Oh, that came from you, did it?' he responded. 'Well, last year we published the salaries for our senior management. That went well, so this year we published them for all our staff. We haven't looked back.'

In 2009 Piscines Ideales was rated the best workplace in Europe among small and medium-sized businesses. I can't claim that moving to transparent salaries was the reason but it certainly doesn't seem to have done any harm.

When asked why they need to keep salaries secret, a surprising number of people respond: 'because they are not fair'. If this is true of your organization, my challenge would be: could you set a date in the future when you will make salaries open, and use that as a target for making your salaries fair?

Questions: If your salaries are not public within your organization, why not?

Would your decisions on salaries be different if you knew everybody would see the figures?

Chapter Six
Recruit for attitude, train for skill

Why most recruitment gets it wrong

Imagine you were in charge of spotting new talent and recruiting players for a successful football club. Obviously what you would normally do is watch them play, to see how good their skills were in practice.

But stop for a moment and imagine you did this job in the same way that most companies do their recruitment. Instead of watching people perform, you would sit them down and get them to talk about how good they were at playing football, about what makes a good footballer and about challenges that they have overcome.

Imagine now that you have two candidates before you: John Motson and David Beckham. John Motson is a British football commentator, who is great at talking about football but has never played the game at a serious level. David Beckham is one of the best footballers of his generation but, especially in his early playing days, could come over as shy and hesitant and not especially articulate.

Clearly if you watched them play there would be only one choice. But if you used the recruitment method used by most companies, getting people to talk about their ability in interviews, you would be likely to end up with John Motson as your new star player.

It is an absurd idea but it is exactly what happens in company recruitment every day. People are tested not on their ability to do a job, but on their ability to talk about it. It is not surprising that a lot of companies end up recruiting the wrong people for the job.

We discovered this early on when recruiting trainers. Again and again we would find trainers saying exactly the right things when they explained what made great training. But the very same trainers who proclaimed the importance of involvement would go on to give a demonstration session in which they delivered a lecture and barely asked a question of their students.

Question: In your recruitment, do you get potential recruits to talk about how they could do the job, or to actually do the job?

Get people to do the job, not talk about it

When we recruit a trainer at Happy we rarely have a one-to-one session at all. Instead we invite the candidates in groups and start the interview by delivering training to them, followed by a discussion of our training style. They then take it in turns to deliver a training session to each other.

The reason we train them is to ensure they are absolutely clear about what is expected of them. (We also send in advance the framework their session will be assessed against, and point them to an example video on our website.) We invite them in groups, partly to enable them to train each other but also to see how they interact. One of our key requirements is that they are positive and supportive of each other, which we can only test if we see them working with others.

At the second interview they again deliver a training session. But after five minutes we take them aside and give them feedback and coaching. They then deliver that part of the session again. This is a crucial test, to see if they can respond to feedback and develop the training skills we need.

A key element we are testing in both interviews is the ability to respond and change. Those who succeed are those who adapt. The result is that experienced IT trainers, who are often set in their ways, rarely get through the interviews. Tracey, our most recent recruit, was convinced she stood no chance when she turned up to an interview and found five experienced trainers who had applied for the job alongside her. She had never trained before. But she got the job because she showed the most potential to train in our style, take initiative and support others.

We don't look at CVs and we don't generally ask people much about their past experience. We are interested in their potential in the future, not their past. And we have worked hard to find a way of evaluating that potential.

You may wonder if this works just as well for senior positions. I would argue that it does. I am Chair of Governors of my local comprehensive school in Hackney, the school my children go to. The most important role of a chair comes when the head teacher moves on and you have to co-ordinate the selection of a new one, and that time duly came round for me.

As governors (including parents, staff and others) we defined carefully what we wanted. And then we set out a range of activities over two days to thoroughly assess the candidates. There were 16 activities in total, but the role of head teacher is very important in a school and it was vital we got the right person.

As well as going before panel interviews, candidates were asked to run a senior management team meeting (not be interviewed by it, but run it), meet with parents and students, attend a governors' meeting, have management meetings with the two most challenging departments and run a full staff meeting. What was interesting was that the candidate who succeeded in the panel interviews, and was able to talk about how well they would do the job, was different from the candidate who succeeded in the exercises that tested their ability to do the job. We, of course, chose the latter – a decision that I believe was vital to the school's future success.

I believe it is possible in all jobs to create activities and tests that mirror what candidates will actually do in the job. It can never be a perfect simulation, but it shows a lot more about the person than a standard interview. I sometimes say, and I'm only half-joking, that if I wanted to recruit a brain surgeon then I'd want to see them cut somebody up in the interview.

Pret A Manger – the real test

Pret A Manger, the successful UK sandwich chain, puts a lot of effort into recruitment – and into training its staff once they are employed. Once a candidate has got through the interview, there is another stage. They spend a day working in one of Pret's shops. At the end of the day the team there votes on whether or not to accept them, and only if they pass that test are they employed.

Questions: *Have you clearly defined the key attributes you are looking for?*

Do your interviews test these attributes by getting candidates to perform tasks as closely related as possible to the real job? If not, how could they do so?

Recruit for attitude, train for skill

I can't claim responsibility for this slogan. I think I first came across it in the writings of management guru Tom Peters. But we have enthusiastically adopted it.

At Happy a core requirement is that people are positive and supportive of others. This is central to the culture of the company and so is required of all staff. That means it is not enough to have strong core skills. You only get rewarded and promoted if you are also seen as being supportive in the office.

Clearly we need to test for this in our recruitment. So, as mentioned before, we never interview people individually.

How would we test how supportive somebody was of others if they are on their own? (Yes, we could ask them to give examples of when they have helped others but you will know that we regard getting people to talk about their abilities as fairly pointless.)

So we interview for all jobs in groups. Typically our interviewees will spend two to three hours with us at their first interview and take part in a range of activities, working with their colleagues. A key element of what we are looking for is their attitude and how they interact with others.

Abel & Cole – getting the right people in the job

Ella Heeks tells the story of how, as Managing Director of Abel & Cole, she recruited the key managers for the buying department. Initially she turned to those experienced in buying groceries, generally people from the big supermarkets. This is a tough business, with companies such as Tesco and Asda working to cut prices paid to suppliers at every turn.

Her first two buyers, Dave and Mike, were experienced and driven and appeared to be doing a great job... until they abruptly left, taking some key suppliers with them, to set up a rival organic box delivery company.

Then she employed Steve, who came with an impressive record of years spent negotiating for Tesco. She realized something was wrong when, working late one night, she overheard angry shouting coming from another office. Ella found Steve bellowing down the phone at one of their key suppliers, over what turned out to be a relatively minor matter.

'I'm sorry. I can't do it,' confessed Steve. 'I can't get out of the way of working of over a decade in the business.' He decided to leave.

Finally Ella turned to Julie. Julie had not been recruited as a buyer, and had no experience in that area. In fact Ella had never been absolutely clear what job she had recruited Julie to do. But her values and commitment fitted so well with the Abel & Cole approach that she went ahead and took her on.

So Julie was a little surprised when Ella asked if she wanted to take over the buying department. She had a lot to learn (and, fortunately, Steve stayed around for a while and taught her some of the tricks of the trade). But, as Ella had realized, Julie embodied the values of Abel & Cole, and that ensured she was a success.

And, in case you were wondering, the company that Dave and Mike set up as a rival did not prosper. It lasted two years before they moved on to other things.[1]

Imagine you are recruiting a technical specialist to support your IT systems. You have two candidates. Tim is a real techie and clearly an expert in your systems. But he is dismissive of others and will be hard to work with. Sreena has less expertise but is keen to learn. Which do you recruit?

We have tried both. There are challenges in having less technical expertise but we found much greater challenges in having somebody on board who wasn't supportive of others. Indeed it threatened the whole culture of Happy, with the message that you could be as nasty as you wanted if your core expertise was strong enough.

'We had that situation,' commented a colleague in a medium-sized retail company. 'We hired somebody who was brilliant technically but their communication and social skills were so poor they needed the virtual full-time attention of one of our managers. They didn't listen well, they didn't communicate what they'd done and they didn't understand the business need. If you absolutely need that specific skill, do take into account the costs of having somebody without the right attitude.'

Sir Stuart Hampson, ex-Chair of UK retailer John Lewis, shares the 'recruit for attitude' approach. He describes how grocery delivery company Ocado select their drivers on attitude. 'The key is the impression the customer will get when they bring the bags into the kitchen. That is what Ocado selects on; they can teach them how to drive.'

Questions: Is the attitude of your staff important to you?

If so, how do you test for attitude in your recruitment? Do you place as much importance on candidates' attitude as on their abilities?

Why do they need a degree?

I am told that at Virgin you are not allowed to require a degree when you recruit somebody. After all, Richard Branson, the company's founder, famously dropped out of school and never went near a university. Clearly, if you work for Virgin, you wouldn't want to use a recruitment method that would exclude your founder.

But then again, even if you don't work for Virgin, why would you want to use a recruitment method that excluded somebody like Richard Branson? Or Bill Gates. Or Steve Jobs. Or Alan Sugar. Or any one of thousands of other talented and successful people who do not have degrees.

Cathy Busani is Managing Director of Happy Computers. Her role at Happy is invaluable and she is responsible, in practice, for a substantial amount of the innovative approaches described in this book. Her skills have been widely recognized. She was voted by *Personnel Today* as HR Manager of the Year, nationwide. She has been a finalist in two competitions for Best UK Boss, one run by the *Daily Telegraph* and the other by the Department of Trade and Industry.

Cathy would not even have been considered for many management jobs, because she doesn't have a degree. She comes from an immigrant family and left school at 16. However, even without those circumstances, she probably wouldn't have gone to university because she isn't particularly academic.

It is true that academic skills are sometimes useful. When I need to pass one of Microsoft's certifications or to complete a government tender, both of which require you to answer complex questions in a very specific way, I will often turn to somebody who has proven to be good at passing exams. For those specific tasks, that skill is very useful. However, for 95 per cent of the work we do, there is little or no match between academic skills and real-life business need.

Talk to any fairly ambitious person who doesn't have a degree and you will hear stories of the frustration they've experienced in not even being considered for jobs they are well suited to. On a recent course one woman told of being the top salesperson in her team at Barclays Mercantile, achieving her annual target after eight months. She left after discovering she couldn't be promoted because the next level required a degree. Another delegate on the course had 15 years of experience of working with socially disadvantaged groups and decided to apply to work in the prison service. His application was not even considered because the website gave him a straight rejection for lacking a degree.

I believe that when people ask for a generic degree (ie they don't mind which subject), they are really saying, 'I'd like to hire somebody like me, from my kind of background' – even if they are not the best person for the job. And the truth is that this approach is highly discriminatory – as black, working-class and disabled people are still hugely under-represented in our universities.

Indeed it could be argued that the insistence on academic qualifications is one of the main barriers to social mobility today. In the 1960s, if you weren't particularly academic, it was possible to rise on ability, as few people went to university, and so few jobs required a degree. Now, barriers to entry for those without degrees are everywhere.

Questions: *Does your recruitment ever ask for a generic degree?*

If so, is there any reason why it should? Can you stop the practice?

Don't rely on qualifications

For some years our finance manager was a young woman called Natalie Day. She joined Happy at the age of 16, straight from school, and was employed in several roles before working her way up to being in charge of our finances. School had never agreed with Nat and she never achieved a maths qualification. In fact she didn't even turn up for her examinations. As a result, for most companies, she would never have been considered for any job in finance, never mind Finance Manager.

But in all her years in the role Natalie never had to calculate the angle on a triangle. Or solve a quadratic equation. Or do even the most basic algebra. These are the kinds of skills tested in maths GCSE, which many organizations make a requirement in recruitment. This is very strange, given that the skills it tests are rarely used in most jobs.

Maths GCSE courses are well designed to develop and test the skills required in a range of subjects at A level and degree level. If you are recruiting somebody to an engineering degree, or to architecture or economics, it makes sense to require a maths GCSE or even maths A level. However, maths GCSEs are not designed or intended to test the skills needed in most workplaces. What I don't understand is that so many companies (especially large ones) still require a maths GCSE – meaning they want a good knowledge of trigonometry and algebra – for anything but very specialist occupations.

Businesspeople regularly complain that qualifications do not prepare people for work or test the skills they need. As I've explained, I think this is true. What I find baffling is that these same businesspeople continue to require candidates to have these qualifications to get a job with their company.

What Natalie was brilliant at was negotiating with suppliers and persuading errant clients to pay their bills. Until she took the job, I regarded it as impossible to persuade the Inland Revenue to agree to a late payment. But Natalie succeeded in doing that on a regular basis and, in the difficult period between 2001 and 2003, this may have made the difference between Happy's extinction and survival. Yet these social skills are not tested in any qualification that I am aware of. (By the way, this was several years after the problems with the management accounting mentioned earlier. That one was entirely my responsibility.)

Even where people do have a qualification, it often says more about their ability to pass tests than their actual skills. When we were recruiting for a network administrator some years ago we did ask for an MCSE qualification, which is the standard Microsoft technical certification.[2] At that time we were still using recruitment agencies and they sent us literally dozens of candidates with the required qualification. It was unclear to us how many of them had managed to achieve their MCSE, as only a few could solve the simple technical test that we set them, representing the real problems they would have to deal with in the job.

There are jobs for which qualifications are required. If I was recruiting a doctor I would want to know they had a degree in medicine. The same level of qualification would be needed for an engineer or an architect. But I would never accept any of those qualifications on their own. Instead I would want to find some way to test the candidate's skills and knowledge.

We never ask for a maths GCSE in our recruitment. But we do need many of our staff to be numerate and so we test them for the real tasks involved in their job (for instance, adding up costs, calculating percentages) in the interview.

Questions: *Do you ask for qualifications in any job you recruit for?*

If so, do you need to? Is there another way to test for the skill you want?

Involve people

Ella Heeks built Abel & Cole from £0.5 million to £20 million and then moved on, all by the age of 30. We worked with Ella over several years. 'One key result of the effect Happy had was less stress for me as we involved our people more,' explains Ella. One example is in recruiting managers. Before, Ella and the company's founder, Keith Abel, would make the appointments on their own. There would then follow several months of worry and uncertainty as they waited for the new manager to start, wondering whether or not they would work out.

Working with Happy, they changed the method, involving all the staff in the decision. They create a range of structured exercises, testing candidates' ability to do the job, in which all the people they will manage take part. All are involved in the decision, and disagreement is rare.

'It took away the months of worry and uncertainty between appointment and them starting work,' explains Ella. 'And, since the staff had been involved in the decision, they were committed to making it work.'

Some companies will involve one or two chosen employees in interviews. That process fulfils one purpose, of getting a viewpoint from the front line or from those who will be managed by this person. However, there is a point to involving as many people as possible. Not only do you get a wider view, but you also get the wider commitment that Ella talked of, and that will help the new appointment to go smoothly. When a new member of staff starts, what could be better than having all the people they work with wanting to make the choice successful?

Questions: When interviewing, do you involve the people who will work with, or be managed by, the person you are recruiting?

How can you change your recruitment system to make sure they are involved?

Make it easy for interested people to apply

Happy's external recruitment costs are virtually zero. Last time we needed trainers, I sent out one e-mail. Within a week we had received 93 applications, completed online without any work on our part. From these we recruited the three trainers we needed.

The reason I can do this is that we have a waiting list of people wanting to hear next time we have a job available. At times this list has contained over 2,000 names. For a company with just 50 staff that's a lot of potential recruits.

When I tell people this, they generally react with admiration and envy, wishing they had a company that so many people wanted to work for. And I hope it is true that a lot of those people are on the list because they really want to work for a company that is a great place to work, that promotes work–life balance and seeks to have a positive effect on the community.

But there is another reason we have such a strong waiting list. The other element, and this seems so obvious that I'm always surprised that more companies don't do it, is to make it easy for people to let you know they want to work for you. On the jobs page of our website, people can leave their e-mail address and explain what type of jobs they might be interested in. We don't ask for names or addresses or anything long and complicated. They just have to leave their e-mail and tick some boxes to indicate the kind of jobs they are looking for.

By placing adverts in the newspaper or on an online site, you are contacting only the people who happen to stumble across that advert at that time. If you place them on your website you are relying on them happening to visit your jobs page during the month when that job is open for application.

In contrast, the people I'd most like to recruit are those who have taken the trouble to check out our website and shown an interest in Happy. The technology isn't complicated. At first we programmed it ourselves, though now we use a neat piece of online software called Sign Up (**www.signup.to**).

Many people respond, 'Oh, we do that, we put all our jobs on the website.' This is NOT what I am talking about. My point is to capture people's interest whenever they visit your site, whether or not you have a relevant vacancy at that moment.

I chair a charity called Antidote, which works to promote emotional literacy in schools, and encouraged them to add a piece of code to their site to enable potential associates to register interest. A year later, when they needed extra resources, they found they had dozens of interested people just waiting to be contacted and interviewed.

Questions: *Is it possible to register interest for a job, at any time, on your website?*

If not, how quickly could you implement the idea?

Find the potential in your lowest-paid staff

Our current finance manager joined Happy as a cleaner.[3] France Gallego is from Colombia and, like many immigrants, took whatever job she could when she came to the UK. Luckily somebody at Happy spotted her potential and she now plays an invaluable role in ensuring that our accounts work.

In most organizations there are talents and skills that are underused. Once you throw away arbitrary barriers based on degrees and other qualifications, these talents can come to light if you look for them. Go out there and see what potential is sitting there with your existing staff.

The same is true at the school where I am a governor, with a remarkably similar example. They discovered that one of the women working as a cleaner was an immigrant who had been a bank manager in Venezuela. She was deployed to work in the finance department, where her support has been invaluable.

It is certain that, all over the UK, there are experienced and talented people who have come to Britain from a vast range of countries and are working in menial jobs. They work as cleaners, in contract catering and in a huge range of other low-paid positions. Some companies know this and keep an eye out for talent among some of their lowest-paid staff. Others don't, and miss out on a big potential resource.

One of our favourite training activities is what we call a Speed Learning Day. Instead of a class of six people spending the day together going through an agreed agenda, the learning is split into 60-minute sessions, and each participant chooses a different learning activity every hour. Some of these are provided by us but others can be contributed by members of staff. A security guard might teach Tai Chi or a psychiatric nurse might take a drama class, based on their interests and skills outside work.

Questions: Have you fully explored the potential of your staff?

In particular have you looked among your lowest-paid staff, especially immigrant labour, for unused potential?

Let people leave well

When I am asked what my biggest mistake was, I am spoilt for choice. But one mistake that often comes to mind is the time in around 1996 when I sacked one of our new recruits and asked him to leave that day. Looking back, I think the problem in David's performance was more to do with our management than his actual ability and attitude. But the real mistake was instructing him to leave like that.

That was how I was treated when I was sacked from a job, and is all too common in organizations. However, it is clear that it is neither in that person's interests nor in yours. And it had a very negative effect on our people and levels of trust in the organization.

I like now to follow the example of McKinsey, one of the world's top management consultancies and incredibly demanding of its people. If you are a consultant and it becomes clear you are not going to make it to partner, they take you aside and explain that you would do better to leave and pursue a career elsewhere.

However, there is no abrupt dismissal. Instead they typically give you six months to find another job, and often help you get a position in one of their client's firms. The result is that ex-McKinsey staff are well spread across major companies and the leading public sector organizations, and all of them think McKinsey is great and treated them really well. It can only help the chances of McKinsey being hired by many of those organizations, as well as boosting the morale of staff who remain, as they know they will be looked after by the company.

This is not how people are often treated. When I briefly worked at IBM, back in 1978, a colleague was told to clear his desk and leave because he had gone for an interview at another company. And I still feel resentment towards the company that arbitrarily sacked me – even though it was over 20 years ago, even though it was the best thing that could have happened to me (leading to the founding of Happy), and even though it is now a customer of ours!

A colleague at the supermarket chain Asda put it very well to me. Until the decision to dismiss somebody is made, the focus is on the company's interests. From the moment that decision is taken, the focus should switch to the interests of the individual and what they need to leave in good shape and well suited to getting a new job elsewhere.

Questions: When you let people go, do you do so in a way that leaves them feeling good about themselves and good about your company?
If not, how could you move towards that?

Notes

1 Names have been changed.

2 Microsoft Certified System Engineer, a standard requirement in many technical jobs.

3 Natalie stepped down from the position after having children. She wanted to work three days a week and have a less demanding job.

Chapter Seven
Celebrate mistakes

One to celebrate

One of our trainers, Darren Andrews, likes to tell the story of a disastrous course he taught in his first month. He came into the smoothie office to report that it hadn't gone well.
I overheard and went up to him and asked him how it went. He explained that he hadn't prepared properly and it had been a disaster. I then gave him a hug and said, 'One to celebrate.'

I wasn't joking. At Happy we want to create an atmosphere where people feel free to experiment, try new things and sometimes get it completely wrong. It was clear Darren was not in denial or blaming somebody else. So within the Happy culture it really was one to celebrate.

Note that I did not feel the need to ask him what he had learnt and what he would do differently next time. Having established that he was taking responsibility for what went wrong I could be confident he could work that out – possibly with colleagues or his co-ordinator.[1] All I wanted to communicate was that I trusted him, I was delighted we'd employed him and I realized that sometimes it all goes wrong. And the fact he'd come straight in to report it meant we could get on with the key task of contacting the learners and putting it right for them.

'The experience was a revelation to me,' explains Darren. 'The freedom to fail, but fail honestly, made me feel confident to go outside my comfort zone and try new things. I know that, as long as I do all that I can, I won't be blamed if it goes wrong.'

Early on in our lives we learn well. Virtually everybody, barring those with specific disabilities, learns to walk and to talk. But, as we grow older, the proportion of us learning key skills falls. Not everybody learns how to read or do basic maths. Here in the UK around 70 per cent of students achieve the government's basic targets at the age of 11 and only just over half achieve the targets for age 16.

I believe the reaction to mistakes plays a part in this. In our earliest years we receive only encouragement. No parent would think of reacting to a toddler with annoyance when they repeatedly try to take a step and fail. Nobody would tell them, 'No, you don't do it like that. Do it like this. Can't you see?'

Encouraged, and with our mistakes celebrated, we take those early steps and speak those first words. But later things change. As we go off to school, both parents and teachers become more judgemental. We learn to avoid making mistakes and, as a result, many learn to be cautious about trying anything new.

Many people are wary when I talk of 'celebrating mistakes'. They accept the importance of a no-blame culture but feel this is going too far. But, with most people, you are tackling decades of inhibition. To recapture people's natural eagerness to experiment and their ability to learn needs a real challenge to the accepted view that mistakes are bad. And to meet the demands of today's rapidly changing society and markets you need more experimenting.

In the old management framework, where the manager was felt to know best, it seemed to make sense that staff shouldn't experiment. The idea was: one brain (to do the thinking) and many pairs of hands (to do the work). To respond to today's fast-changing environment, we need many active brains and many pairs of hands, and that means everybody gets to experiment.

Go make mistakes

When I started out in business, a key mentor gave me this simple direction: 'Go make mistakes.' And I did, learning as I went. Indeed, it is impossible to be a successful entrepreneur without getting a lot wrong. If you want your people to innovate and try new approaches I encourage you to give them the same direction. And to celebrate when they do get it wrong.

We know that many of the world's greatest innovations came from mistakes. Penicillin was discovered when Alexander Fleming accidentally left his bacterial cultures out when he went away on holiday. The pacemaker resulted from Wilson Greatbatch accidentally using the wrong resistor (of one megaohm strength instead of the planned 10,000 ohms) when inventing a measuring device.

Charles Goodyear invented vulcanized rubber (used in tyres and hundreds of other goods) after spilling a mixture of rubber, sulphur and lead on a hot stove. Coca Cola was the result of Atlanta pharmacist John Pemberton's failed attempt to make a headache remedy.[2] Thomas Edison would never have invented the light bulb if he had not been prepared to fail thousands of times before finding the carbon filament that worked. He is widely quoted as saying, 'I didn't fail 3,000 times. I found 3,000 ways how not to create a lightbulb.'

Questions: What would be different in your organization if mistakes were encouraged and welcomed?

How would it feel next time you make a mistake to openly say, 'Yes, that was me. I got it wrong'?

Mistakes are good

Imagine you have a new recruit who is at the end of their three-month probationary period. They say to you, 'In the time I've been here I have made no mistakes.' How would you feel? Would you want to confirm them in post?

I suspect that, like me, you would find that statement very worrying. Either they weren't being honest, or we hadn't created a good enough environment for them to be open. Or, worst of all, they had made no mistakes – because that would mean they had not tried anything new.

When Microsoft established their research centre in Cambridge, the director was reportedly told: 'If everything you do succeeds, you will have failed.' Think about it. The reason is clear. If everything succeeded then they were obviously not taking enough risks or really trying to create new technologies. (At one of my talks somebody from Microsoft reported that they certainly were succeeding on that measure: 90 per cent of their projects to date had been failures! The key question is the impact of the other 10 per cent.)

It is obvious how that approach is necessary for the frontiers of technology. But I would argue it is equally true of front-line staff in my business. If everything they do succeeds, then it seems unlikely that they are trying new approaches or taking risks to serve the customer better.

Mistakes are good. Mistakes are how we learn. If no mistakes are being made, then are people trying hard enough?

Learning to roller skate

Some years ago I bought in-line skates for my two daughters. And, wanting to join in the fun, I bought a pair for me too. For the girls I made sure they had the full set of padding so that they would be safe. For me, I missed that bit out. Well, I didn't want to look silly! Guess who learnt to skate more quickly?

You won't be surprised to learn that the girls did much better. Some time later, when I was still having to grab at lamp-posts to stop myself, I came across somebody who taught people how to roller skate. The first lesson was always the same: how to fall over. Indeed the learner never went on to the next lesson until the tutor was confident they knew how to fall over safely. Once they had mastered that, they would be able to learn properly – without fear of getting it wrong.

I see my roller-skating story as a parable for how to learn generally. If it is not possible to fail safely, then there will be a limit on what people are prepared and able to try. By 'fail safely', I mean it has to be possible to fail without damaging the person or the organization.

Questions: *What are the consequences of getting it wrong in your organization?*

How can you ensure people can experiment, fail and learn – safely?

No blame even for big mistakes: Huntsman and the big red button

Huntsman Petrochemicals is a chemical company in Middlesbrough in the north-east of England. At Huntsman there was apparently a big red button on the wall in the administration offices. If you pressed the button, then the chemicals were discharged into the local river. As you can imagine, this was only for an emergency situation and it was not a good idea to press it.

One day the company had scaffolders in and one of the contractors was walking through this section of the company, carrying his scaffold pole on his shoulders. You've probably guessed what happened next. As he passed the big red button his scaffolding pole nudged it, setting off the discharge.

When they heard what had happened, his scaffolding company sacked him. But what was interesting was the reaction of Huntsman. They not only insisted he be reinstated, they also insisted he be sent back to work at their site and held a ceremony to thank him.

You may wonder why. The reason is the reaction of the scaffolder when he realized what he'd done. He could have simply carried on and nobody would have known it was his fault. Instead he ran into the control room and explained that he seemed to have set off some sort of reaction. As a result the discharge was stopped quickly, damage was very limited and no environmental fine was incurred. If he hadn't done that, it could have taken 24 hours to find the cause and solve the problem.

The story spread like wildfire around Huntsman, as it was intended to. Staff got the message that this was a no-blame company. If people took responsibility they would be supported, even when they got things wrong.

There are mistakes that are part of the learning process but there are also mistakes, as in this example, which you really do not want to happen. But it is the cover-up of a mistake that is normally far more damaging than the mistake itself. If one of my people messes up with our biggest client, and comes and tells me about it straight away, I can almost certainly rescue the situation. If I weren't to hear for a couple of weeks, and then only from the client, it could be too late to remedy.

The other key point about a no-blame culture is that it makes it easier to find the real problems and solve them. In the case of Huntsman the actual problem was clear, that it was far too easy to press the big red button by accident. If you are looking for whose fault something was, then you can easily miss what really needs changing. The question should not be 'who did that?', but what in the system, or in staff training, allowed it to happen.

There is a difference between blame and responsibility. The celebration is the next stage after a person takes responsibility and says, 'I got it wrong.' That taking of responsibility is especially crucial in jobs where life-and-death situations can occur.

You need a process for this. One delegate from a bank commented that they were very good at responding to a specific problem by sending a lovely bunch of flowers to say sorry. But they ended up sending out dozens of bouquets every week for the same mistake and the underlying problem never got fixed.

At Happy we have a monthly 'trouble-shoot' meeting. This brings together all the feedback we collect and focuses on what's gone wrong in the last month. The aim is simply to work out what changes are needed, normally to the systems we use, to make sure it is unlikely to happen again.

Questions: *Does your culture encourage people to take responsibility for a mistake, knowing they won't be blamed?*

As importantly, do you have a system for tracking problems and fixing them permanently?

Notes

1   The co-ordinator is the closest we come to a line manager at Happy. Their role is to support, motivate and coach our people.

2   *Top ten accidental inventions*, Science Channel: http://tinyurl.com/nhujp7.

Chapter Eight
Community: create mutual benefit

Profits are important and necessary but not sufficient

To be honest I've never been motivated by the idea of owning a fast car, a Rolex watch, a huge mansion or many of the other material things that we are encouraged to desire. (Though an expensive super-light carbon-fibre bicycle, that is a different matter.)

In the early days, I wasn't very focused on profit at all. My aim was to grow the business and increase our impact. Then, in 2001, the IT training industry plunged into recession, with sales across the sector falling by 30 per cent.

Happy had invested heavily in e-learning, and we were already at the limits of our overdraft. We survived, but only just. It involved weekly discussions with the bank manager and I shall never forget the month that the bank refused to allow salaries to be paid.

It was a lesson I should have learnt at *News on Sunday*, the radical newspaper I helped to found in 1987. One of the investors was Alec Horsley, founder of Northern Foods. (His son, Nick Horsley, was Chair of the company.)

I remember he was part of a group of investors we were showing round the company a month before launch. One of my colleagues was explaining the finances and said, 'The break-even is sales of 800,000 copies a week.'

This outraged Alec. Though he was 85 years old at the time, he grabbed my colleague by the lapels and forcefully stated, 'Break-even is not the point. Don't you dare talk about break-even. The aim of a business is to make a profit.'

He was right. A business can only survive and prosper by making a profit. It needs reserves for the hard times, it needs investment to research and innovate, and founders and investors need to be rewarded. I often give talks to students from the School for Social Entrepreneurs in London and am always inspired by the range of imaginative proposals for companies that will bring real benefit to communities.

But I always stress that they should never forget the importance of making a profit. They may want to mentor East End teenagers, set up job opportunities for the most disenfranchized, enable ex-offenders to find work, or many other great schemes. But to have the impact they want, they must make a profit.

However if that is the only focus, then one has to ask: why are you in business? What will you look back on with pride in 30 years' time as your achievement? Having a positive impact on society needn't be a cost. With the right attitude, it can make your business better and stronger.

Question: Are you clear on both the social benefit of what you do, and the need to make a financial return?

I'm in business to make a profit. Of course I am. But I'm also in business to make a difference. Otherwise what is the point?

Increase the impact of your skills and resources

'Africa is amazing: we saw the gorillas, the tree-climbing lions, loads of hippos, elephants and many more. Working in Africa is very interesting. Things don't always work out, constantly have to be re-planned, negotiated again and adjusted. It's a lot of fun, though! My negotiation skills have improved big time. We had no power today and had to improvise a learner-focused, hands-on MS Word training session without using the computer. It worked!

It is all very hilarious and creative and exciting! Nicky and I are living in a little village without internet café, or shop and the house has neither electricity nor running water. Our host family is so sweet and welcoming. I wish you could experience all this.'

This was the e-mail from Nicole Kollermann, one of the Happy trainers who went out to Uganda to work with a local charity. Our role was to train up their people to be great trainers, so leaving a sustainable centre, training to the highest standards.

Indeed, while proofing this book, Nicole added: 'I learnt *so* much through our Uganda experience. It shaped my opinions about development aid and how we give to society in a major way. It was a huge education experience.'

To be honest, we started on this route from fairly selfish reasons. We noticed one year that most of the staff who had left Happy had done so to travel, to see the world. We wondered if it might be possible to meet that need while keeping them at Happy. Could we find projects in the third world for them to get involved in that would satisfy their wanderlust and bring real local benefit?

So trainers have gone to different projects in Uganda, Northern Nigeria and Cambodia. In each case we work with a locally based charity and seek to have a permanent impact. Our trainers report back that they have had one of the best experiences of their lives, living with a local family and experiencing a culture in a way a traveller – with few local contacts – rarely can.

This is one example of making the most of our resources, in this case our training skills. Another is in making the most of the written resources we have produced.

A journalist once asked me how we protect our intellectual property. My answer was that we give it away for free on our website. All our manuals, the copyright element of our work, are available for download and are free for individual use. Businesses and most other organizations pay a licence fee if they want to use the manuals across their organizations, but state schools can use them and adapt them for free.

This was the result of looking at how we could have most impact with our resources. Now we give 4 per cent of our profits away in cash to charities we support. But we are a small organization and we know the impact of this is always going to be limited. So we sat down and thought about how we could increase the impact of our resources.

One example was trainers going out to Africa, not to train people directly in Word, Excel and so on, as this would have limited impact. Instead the aim was to train local workers to be great trainers, and provide them with resources to help them do a great job.

Another example is the free use of our manuals in schools. It costs us very little, just the cost of setting up and administering the website, but has a huge impact in providing hundreds (if not thousands) of teachers across the UK, and beyond, with resources to help them do a great job.

Questions: Which of your resources could be of real benefit in the community?

How can you increase their impact?

'I milked a goat': mutual benefit

We have a policy at Happy that 10 per cent of profits is given back to the community. Of this, 4 per cent is given in cash and the remainder is in kind, in the form of work carried out for free by our staff. When I am asked what the motivation for our philanthropy is, I answer that it is not philanthropy. We do this because it makes Happy more effective as a business.

We have a timebank for work in kind, currently set at 100 days a year. The idea is that any member of staff can claim days from the timebank. So, instead of everybody having three days a year (and many people not using them), somebody who is good at finding projects might use up 30 days and another person use up none.

There are three criteria: first, the project must have a benefit to the community, obviously. Second, it must also have a benefit to Happy. Third, it must have a significant impact on the organization we work with. (This is intended to encourage people to work with small charities, for whom our work can make a real difference.)

The concept is 'mutual benefit'. The idea is that we can sustain this relatively high level of community work, providing it brings benefit to Happy as well as to the community. The most common benefit is increased motivation for our people and development of their skills.

This was clear in the Uganda project. We could have sent Nicole and Nicky on a personal development course, which might actually have cost more and had less impact. Instead we gave them a project with many challenges – such as teaching IT during a 24-hour power cut – but also with real meaning. There are major commercial companies who do similar activities as part of their development of key managers but I would emphasize it is fully possible for a small business like ours too.

We sometimes find that our trainers have to train in something such as web development or database design in which they have relatively little experience. In the past we might have set up a dummy project to give them the practice they needed. Now we try to pair them up with a local charity that genuinely needs this work, and where possible make sure that a more experienced person is available here to coach our person and make sure the work is done well.

The benefit is in experience in a real-world application, but also in getting out of the office and doing something different. Georgie had been a trainer with Happy for many years and had done consistently great work. But I will never forget how motivated he was by a five-day project developing a website for an inner city farm, set up to provide experiences for local children who never went to the countryside. Afterwards I asked him what he got from it. He looked at me and said excitedly, 'I milked a goat!'

The scheme is targeted at small local charities and currently benefits around 40 organizations a year. Another example was the Markfield Project, set up by parents in Haringey (north London) to support autistic children and those with learning difficulties. Our trainer Darren Andrews explains:

> To be honest, I wasn't looking forward to it. My mother died 10 months ago and this would have been her birthday. When I got there it turned out to be one of the staff's birthdays and there was some confusion – kids kept coming in giving me a hug and wishing me Happy Birthday.
>
> But it became one of the best days I've ever had at Happy. The work Markfield do is amazing. But they had been spending days each month extracting information from their database to report to funders. After what I set up, they just click a button and they get all the reports they need. It was a great challenge, including a query on a query on a query on a query. I worked out new ways of reporting and it really appealed to the geek in me.

Other training providers express admiration for this charity work and ask how we can afford to do it. My question back is how they can afford not to do it. Apart from the benefits to the community, the gains in staff motivation, in community goodwill and in staff development far outweigh – in my view – the costs in staff time. Given the opportunity of having a company with these great resources, why would you not want to do work like this?

Questions: Is your community work designed to be purely philanthropic or to bring mutual benefit?

If it did bring mutual benefit, could it be expanded far beyond its current level?

Would anybody notice...

There are some great examples of companies getting involved in their communities, and there are some lousy ones. One test I like to use is this:

Would anybody notice if this scheme was cancelled?

If your company's contribution consists of the chairman giving a cheque once a year to the charity of his or her choice, then nobody would particularly notice if it didn't happen next year. Equally the practice in some companies of allocating 1 per cent to charity and setting up a separate department to give it out would affect only those few people if it got cancelled.

A good scheme should engage and excite your people. At my children's primary school in Hackney a convoy of black cabs arrived once a week at the gates. Out of the taxis stepped besuited consultants from city finance firm JP Morgan.

I have to admit that many of the parents, including myself, were doubtful of the benefit of these city types descending on our inner-city school. But actually it soon turned out that the children really enjoyed their sessions and looked forward to them. And it was very popular among the JP Morgan staff, for some of whom it was the highlight of the week. It would certainly be noticed if that project got cancelled.

Question: Do you have projects which actively involve your people in the community, or do they consist of doing work on their behalf?

Corporate social responsibility should be about everything you do

Some years ago I was invited to speak to an organization called the Social Responsibility Group (SRG), on the topic of 'How to get more small businesses involved in corporate social responsibility'. The SRG was made up of people from large corporations and my answer to the question was simple: 'Set a better example.'

I knew that many of the organizations in the room allocated an amount, normally 1 per cent of profits, to charitable work. I knew that this amounted to millions for some companies and that they had some excellent programmes.

However, as I looked around the room, I saw companies that I knew treated their staff badly and required long hours of work. I saw companies that paid their suppliers late, almost as a policy. I saw companies that claimed to follow equal opportunities but whose senior staff were entirely white, male and of middle-class backgrounds. I saw companies whose core product was bad for people and bad for the environment. And I saw one company that spent far more on advertising the good work it did than on the good work itself.

I am reminded of a cartoon in a UK newspaper that showed a huge mining company despoiling the earth, but their protective helmets were made from recycled plastic. I am often reminded of that when I read of companies whose core activity is damaging (like British American Tobacco below) but that use 'corporate social responsibility' to put a nice marketing gloss on things. The key question is whether ethics are at the heart of the company's decisions, or just an add-on to make the company feel or look good.

The biggest impact most companies have on society is through the products they sell, the people they employ and the suppliers they buy from. And, of course, the effect on the environment of producing their products. If you are really committed to having a positive effect on society, that is where to start.

British American Tobacco – positive social impact?

In the late 1990s, British American Tobacco approached one of the top five UK consultancies about helping them with a programme of social responsibility to improve their image, and also to improve their positive impact on society.

To its credit the consultancy responded by saying that they would be happy to help as long as BAT was prepared to start by dropping its main product, tobacco. As a result, the work did not happen.

There are examples of major corporations that have changed. One of the most inspiring is the carpet corporation Interface and its Chief Executive, Ray Anderson. His conversion moment came in 1997, when he was asked to give a talk on the environment to sales staff. His first reaction was simply to state, 'We obey the law', the standard defence of corporations across the world.[1]

Reading up for his talk, he underwent a transformation: 'I was running a company that was plundering the earth. I thought, "Damn, some day people like me will be put in jail!"' The company set itself the mission of becoming a 'restorative enterprise', with a positive effect on the environment, by 2020.

Interface's definition of this goal does not lack ambition: 'To be the first company that, by its deeds, shows the entire industrial world what sustainability is in all its dimensions. People, process, place and profits – by 2020 – and in doing so we will become restorative through the power of influence.'[2]

The programme has brought direct financial benefits. The waste-elimination programme alone has resulted in $433 million of savings for the company.[3] But the key lesson is that, whatever company we work for or run, we have a choice. We can decide to have a positive effect on the world.

Questions: If ethics really were at the core of decision-making in your organization, what would be different?

What can you do to make clear to your people that your company has strong ethical values?

Notes

1 'Executive on a mission: saving the planet':
New York Times, 22 May 2007.

2 Interface press release, 23 March 2010.

3 Ray Anderson died in August 2011 but Interface
continues to seek to be a truly sustainable company.

Chapter Nine
Love work, get a life

Keep people to their hours

Before my children were born I rarely left the office before 8 pm and normally went in on Sundays too. My wife was doing an MBA, as well as a full-time job, and so we shared a workaholic lifestyle. That changed when our first child was born, and I wanted to be home in time for an early dinner and do my share of cooking it.

As a result I was working two hours less each day. But, strange as it seemed then, I wasn't getting any less done. When I'd known I could work into the evening there was far less urgency. Now I was much more focused.

Many businesses regard working late as a sign of commitment. It is just as likely to be a sign of poor organization, or of too many meetings and unnecessary activities during the day. One consultant I know reckons, on average, he can reduce working time by at least eight hours a week for those working in large companies – principally by removing the unproductive activity.

And the more hours you work, the less effective you can be. If I go to see a doctor about something serious, I don't want to see a junior doctor who is at the end of a 20-hour shift and has had no sleep recently. I want to see a doctor who is well rested, refreshed and alert.

The same goes for meeting a lawyer or a designer or even the waiter in the local restaurant. Or a trainer. One of the things our clients comment on is that our staff are so friendly and relaxed. The truth is that long hours and stressful jobs do not make for great customer interaction, great service or great decisions.

Salina Gani, Learning & Development Manager at Paul (the bakery chain), backed up this view:

> The most productive time of my life has been the time I've worked fewer hours. I used to feel guilty if I left at 6.30, and that was my official leave time. I worked long hours and it made me ill.
>
> What changed? A new manager who didn't expect those hours. My job is to identify my workload and get it done. I manage my own time. I'm happier, I'm less stressed and I just get more done. My manager says I do the equivalent of several times what she's seen others do at other firms.

There are times when project deadlines require long hours. But if we find one of our staff is working over their core hours (yes, that means working over 38 hours) on a frequent basis, our priority is to help them to reduce those hours.

When President Clinton got it wrong

When asked what advice he would give to incoming President Barack Obama, President Clinton responded:

It's important to preserve your family life. It's important to be a good parent. It's important to take some time off. In my long political career, most of the mistakes I made, I made when I was too tired, because I tried too hard and worked too hard. And I think that preserving a balance so that you're always fresh is important... you make better decisions when you're not too tired. So that would be my only advice.[1]

Clinton was known for his workaholic nature and his determination to work late into the night. But even of him, it seems that he felt this reduced his effectiveness. (And, no, I don't know if he celebrated those mistakes...)

I know that the time when I worked my longest hours was at *News on Sunday*, as it headed towards disaster. This was also when I was least effective. Eventually I had to be ordered to take a holiday. It was probably the best management instruction I ever received and I returned refreshed and more effective.

You will have gathered from this book that our culture is not generally one of instruction. But this is one area where we make an exception. If one of our people has got trapped in a cycle of long hours and overwork, we do sometimes simply order them to stop – while seeking to provide whatever support is necessary to enable this.

Questions: If your people work beyond their hours, are they doing so effectively?

What would be different if people had to stick to their core hours?

It's not about you, it's about them

Let us look at flexible working. Under what circumstances would you agree to somebody working flexibly? Here are some possible requests:

- An employee wishes to take Mondays off to look after their baby and work their hours over the rest of the week. Would you agree to it?

- An employee wishes to take Monday off to do a part-time degree (not work related) and again work their hours over the rest of the week. Would you agree to it?

- An employee wants to take Monday off because they are normally exhausted after a hard night's clubbing on Sunday. They propose to work their hours over the rest of the week. Would you agree to it?

Some organizations find it hard to allow people to work flexibly at all and will reject all three. Most people respond, though, by saying they would agree to the baby example. Around half generally agree to the degree study. But very few agree to the clubbing request.

That third example is a real one. We had a member of staff whose favourite club was on a Sunday night. He would either turn up exhausted on Mondays or not come in at all. Attempts to get him back on track were proving difficult, he was becoming demotivated and we were heading towards disciplinary action.

Then his co-ordinator came up with the idea of him working a 'compressed week' across Tuesday to Friday. This meant he would work longer days, fulfilling his 38 hours in those four days. It was a win-win solution. He was delighted and became strongly motivated again. We got the benefit of a dedicated and skilled member of staff working to his potential.

Flexible working is not about what you approve of, but about the member of staff and what they need. It is not about you. It is about them. When companies give flexible working to only certain staff, such as parents of young children, it causes resentment among others. This is easily avoided by leaving the decision on what matters to the staff themselves, rather than setting yourself up as the judge.

So how do you work out who can work which hours, given that there will inevitably be conflicts? Our solution is simple. Again, don't set yourself up as judge and jury. Instead leave it to the staff themselves.

When we first started encouraging flexible working, there were all sorts of requests from the 'smoothie' department, which was responsible for all incoming bookings and enquiries as well as a range of other tasks.[2] So we said to them, 'You decide.' We set the parameters, agreeing that the company needed two people on the phones every day from 9 am to 5.30 pm and one person on reception from 9 am to 11 am each morning (when our students arrive). Also everybody should be in on Tuesdays to enable a full staff meeting to take place.

Within those parameters the team could agree their hours. The compressed week was popular, as was going home early on Fridays. But overall everybody got more or less what they wanted. And because several people chose to come in early, the result was that there is normally somebody in the office from 7 am and the phones are answered well before 9 am. Again, everybody benefited.

Now even at Happy people can't work whatever hours they want. Our training, for instance, is generally delivered from 10 am to 5 pm, so trainers can't work part-days. You rarely have to spell out things like that. People know what is practical. We don't say you can have whatever flexible working you want. But we do start from the assumption that the proposal makes sense. The onus is on the company to prove it won't work (though we never have needed to) rather than on the individual to prove it will.

I am often staggered by the response at other companies to requests for flexible working. One competitor was trying hard to persuade its training manager to return from maternity leave. Yet, when she said she wanted to work a four-day week, they said no – losing a key member of staff.

A friend at one of the UK's leading consultancies also asked to work a four-day week after returning from maternity leave. She was told, 'Yes, you can. But of course it means you won't get promoted again.' Naturally she left, moving on to very successful senior roles at more flexible organizations.

Contrast this with inspirational entrepreneurs like Karen Mattison and Emma Stewart, who set up their award-winning company, Women Like Us, on the basis of matching women who wanted to work only during school hours with companies that needed part-time workers.

Questions: Do you have rigid rules on what hours and days people can work, or is your organization flexible to people's needs?

What would be different if the onus was on your company to prove an approach would not work, rather than on the employee to prove it would?

Find 'me' time

The most common use of flexible working is to enable you to spend more time with your family, especially when you have young children. One result of this can be simply to change the source of your exhaustion – you are worn out from looking after the kids instead of from long hours at work.

It was our Managing Director Cathy Busani who introduced me to the concept of 'me' time. Cathy doesn't work on Mondays, but it isn't to look after children. Instead she will typically treat herself to a shopping trip or pamper herself with a manicure or massage. She makes sure she gets 'me' time. The result is she returns to work on Tuesday feeling great, and we get the benefit in her work.

Cathy does an exercise where you take a plan of the week and fill in all your commitments in different colours. The key question is whether you get enough time to do what you really enjoy, what rejuvenates you and enables you to work at your best.

I enjoy work and I love spending time with my family. But the other activity that gives me real fulfilment is cycling. Taking Cathy's guidance, I increasingly found time to cycle. I also found a fellow entrepreneur with the same interests. Every few months we would go off on a day's business book cycle. We stopped frequently at cafés to read a chosen business book. And then cycled through the countryside, or along canal towpaths, discussing the ideas and our plans for business.

This led to me taking on the biggest physical challenge of my life. In the summer of 2008 I entered for the *étape*, the public stage of the Tour de France. Over 7,000 entrants cycle up two of the toughest climbs in the Pyrenees, chased by a 'broom wagon' that sweeps you off the road if you are not quick enough. Getting to the peak of the Tourmalet and the Hautacam has left a determination, a renewed belief that if I really put my mind to a challenge, I can achieve it.

Where have you got your best ideas?

This question was asked of a group of over 200 managers at a Common Purpose gathering I attended in London. Some answered 'in the shower', others said it was during physical activity or on holiday. But what was striking was that virtually nobody said they got their best ideas at work.

Giving yourself 'me' time is a route not only to feeling more refreshed but also to giving yourself a chance to reflect and get better ideas.

Questions: Do you get 'me' time in your life?

What would 'me' time mean for you? What would give you extra fulfilment? How can you fit it into your life?

Notes

1 Clinton speech: http://bit.ly/a3YPHx.

2 As explained earlier, 'smoothie' stands for smooth operator and is our name for our administration team. The team chose it in the early nineties after dancing to the Sade song at a nightclub.

Chapter Ten
Select managers who are good at managing

Our most radical concept...

Imagine you have a great programmer in your IT department. She has been there for 10 years and does consistently good work. What will happen to her? Most likely she will one day be promoted to Programming Manager. The logic appears to be that the fact that she is a great coder will mean that she is great at supporting and coaching people.

That would never happen at Microsoft, for instance. If they have great programmers, they will make sure they are well paid. They will involve them in key decisions. They will make sure they feel valued. But they won't put them in charge of other people, unless that is something they are really good at. They recognize the truth of what I often describe as Happy's most radical belief:

People should be chosen to manage people...

... on the basis of how good they are at managing people.

This should be a statement of the obvious. But in most companies, you don't get to be a manager because you are good at managing people. You get to be a manager because you are good at your core job, whether it is programming, or accounts, or sales, or administration, or whatever. Or because of length of service. It is assumed that you can *learn* how to manage people well.

When people are promoted to manage others, they are taking on a crucial responsibility. They can make the difference between whether their people feel motivated and look forward to going into work, or dread it. Yet it is rare for an organization, before making somebody a manager, to check if managing people is something that person is likely to be good at.

At Happy we take a different approach. We have department heads who are elected by the staff in that area, and have responsibility for strategic issues for those departments. Separately we have 'co-ordinators', whose responsibility is to support and challenge people on a one-to-one basis, playing the people management role. Some people do both, but many don't.

What this means is that anybody at Happy who manages people has been chosen because we feel they have the potential to be great at managing.

Questions: Are your managers chosen because they have the potential to be great at managing people, or because of their skills in their core job?

How can you make sure all your people have a manager who brings out the best in them?

The two roles of managers

If you ask a group of managers whether they enjoy managing people, you will get two sets of responses. Some respond that they love it. It is what motivates them to come to work. Seeing their people develop and supporting them to reach their potential is an important (sometimes the most important) part of their job.

But there is a large group of managers who give a different response. They are good at the core job but they don't feel they are great at managing people. Indeed the worries of management are what cause them stress and keep them awake at night. These managers are the ones who, in turn, leave their staff feeling demotivated and cause people to leave the company.

Look for a moment at this list of the core skills required of managers:

- strategy;
- decision-making;
- supporting;
- challenging;
- coaching.

Is this a sensible combination of skills, or is there something odd about it? I believe that this list is a combination of two very different skill sets:

Role A	Role B
strategy	supporting
decision-making	challenging
	coaching

People are most likely to be promoted on the basis of their skill in Role A. But if we really believe 'people are our greatest asset' then Role B is just as crucial.

I believe the fault at the heart of management in most organizations is the expectation that people who are good at Role A can be just as good at Role B. Because those Role B skills are really easy to learn, aren't they? For me that assumption is no more sensible than saying, 'Karen is great at repairing cars. So let's get her to do the accounts.'

The world is not divided into people who are good at doings things and people who aren't. People have different skills and abilities. If you want to make the most of the potential in your organization, a key element is to help your people play to their strengths.

Questions: *Are your managers chosen because they are good at managing people, or because they are good at their core job?*

Is it possible to create separate paths for promotion, to ensure some can get promoted without having to manage people?

Build on strengths not weaknesses

Here's a challenge. Let us say that you have two sales-people but you can only afford to send one on a course. Both have been with you for 10 years. One brings in £200,000 a year and the other brings in just £50,000. If the aim is to bring the maximum benefit to the company, who do you send on the course?

Your first impulse may have been to send the person selling just £50,000, who clearly needs help and development. But, if you want the most return on your investment in training, you are likely to get a far bigger increase in sales from the one already performing well.

The concept behind this comes from Marcus Buckingham and his StrengthsFinder analysis with Gallup. In many of their surveys they ask the question, 'At work today, did you get to do what you do best?' They have asked this of over a million people. Only around 20 per cent say yes.[1]

It is common at appraisals to look at people's strengths and weaknesses. The next step is often to work out a way to help them improve in their area of weakness. This may mean going on courses, receiving support, mentoring or other methods. However, there is another approach: get people to spend more time on what they are good at, and less time where they are weak.

Buy the book *Now, Discover Your Strengths*, which includes a free online survey that reveals your five greatest strengths. One of mine is 'Woo' (Win Over Others). This means I am great at networking and meeting people. This is true. I love greeting strangers at corporate exhibitions. I love going to events where I meet new people.

Another of the 33 strengths in the book is 'Relator', the ability to build long-term relationships. For years I beat myself up over my failure to follow up on the new people I met. At the same time I would be frustrated by colleagues I took to exhibitions and other events, and who were hesitant to approach people they didn't know.

The alternative is to get each of us to play to our strengths. I do the meeting and greeting, along with colleagues who are good at that. Others, whose strength is Relator, follow up and build the long-term relationships. Not only are we all happier, but we are all more effective too.

Here is another example. Imagine your child comes home from school with their report card. Reading through it, you find they got three As (English, Maths and History), a C (Biology) and an F (French). Which grade do you focus on? Buckingham asked this question of thousands of people across several countries and found that the majority focused on the F grade. In the United States 77 per cent focused on the weak area. (In the UK it was lower, but still a majority, at 52 per cent.)

You may feel that some attention may be needed on the French but the question was worded quite carefully, to look at emphasis: 'Which of these grades would you spend the most time discussing with your son or daughter?'

There is another way. It is okay to congratulate them on how well they have done in their strong subjects. Instead of getting them to focus on improving in the subject where they got the F, a better strategy may be to work out how to make sure they avoid the weak subject.

We came across StrengthsFinder because we were told it is used extensively by Microsoft. They want to know what their people are good at and how to get them to focus on those areas.

There is a substantial group of managers who will tell you that they don't like managing people, and that they don't feel they are any good at it. One route is to give them development and training. If they are motivated to develop these skills, and want to be good at supporting people, this may work. However, there are many for whom managing people is simply not a strength and will never be. And those are likely to be the same managers who people do not like being managed by and may even leave the company to get away from.

Questions: Do you focus more on helping people to play to their strengths, or on fixing their weaknesses?

Do you make sure that for those who are managing, managing people is one of their strengths?

Find an alternative route to promotion

I love my job... but not my manager

Imagine one of your most valued members of staff comes to you and says, 'I love my job. I love the people I work with. I am even happy with what I am being paid. But I can't stand my manager.' What do you do? How do you solve this problem?

In many companies there would be one of two outcomes: either the manager or the member of staff would leave. At Happy we can solve it in around five minutes. We simply find the person a different manager (or 'co-ordinator' as we call them).

This is possible because we have separated the role of co-ordinator from any fixed-line management hierarchy. We choose co-ordinators according to who is good at supporting and coaching people, the Role B described earlier in this chapter. Separately we have a group of departmental heads, who are chosen because of their ability to see the big picture and take strategic decisions, Role A described above.

The departmental heads are normally elected by the people who work there. It would be nice to say that we do this out of a belief in democracy in the workplace, but this isn't the real reason. We do it because it is more effective. As they say at WL Gore, the remarkable company behind Gore-Tex™, 'If you want to be a leader you had better find some followers.'

One company we worked with had a brilliant marketing director who we shall call Alison. Alison's marketing ability was second to none and those skills were highly valued in the company. However, she wasn't great at management and there was a high staff turnover in the department.

The company wanted to keep Alison's marketing expertise but needed to find a way for her people to feel valued and motivated. Within a traditional hierarchy it is hard to find a solution. But step outside that fixed approach and the solution is easy. We worked with the company to establish Alison as a Senior Marketing Consultant with no management responsibilities. They looked within the marketing team for somebody with good people skills to become the manager.

Once again, the solution is win–win. Alison was delighted, as she got to spend all her time working on what she was good at, in areas she enjoyed and for which she received recognition. She no longer had to cope with people management, which for her was extremely stressful. And the members of the marketing team were also delighted, because they now had a manager who supported them and made them feel good.

My colleague Nicole Kollermann, who is German, explained to me that some of the largest German companies now have two promotion tracks, one for people management and one for technical managers, enabling people to play to their strengths. Lufthansa, for instance, gives the options of a 'management career' or an 'expert career' (*Expertenlaufbahn*). This approach can also be found at Porsche, Siemens and Salzgitter Flachstahl.

There are indeed many companies that have found a way to do this. IBM has long had IBM Fellows. Colleagues at BT and Microsoft tell me that it is certainly possible there to take on a senior role without managing people.

Questions: Is people management the only route to promotion in your organization?

How can you create an alternative career route for people who are great at the core job, but are never going to be great at managing people?

Let people choose their manager

The role of managers is to help people perform at their best. Their job is to support, coach and challenge. We all know from personal experience that some managers are great at this, and that others aren't.

Bad management undermines morale, creates stress, reduces productivity and causes companies to lose some of their best people. It is a massive problem, but there is a simple solution: let people choose their managers. If they don't like the one they've got now, let them decide who they want instead.

Check out some of the research: the evidence is strong that one of the most common reasons for people leaving a job, if not the most common, is to get away from the manager. For example, a study from CMI (the Chartered Management Institute in the UK) found that 47 per cent of respondents left their last role because they were badly managed.[2] People see their manager as very important to them. The CMI study found that 49 per cent would be prepared to take a pay cut if it meant working with a better manager.

At some of the best companies to work for, that simply isn't necessary. At WL Gore, staff (or partners as they call themselves) can choose their manager from anybody in the company. At Happy you can choose your 'co-ordinator' and change them if you would prefer somebody else.

When, at a recent awards ceremony, the host mentioned that at Happy people chose their managers, the audience erupted into a spontaneous round of applause. People know it makes sense. People can see that it would make their lives better, and more productive, if they could choose the right manager for themselves.

In a traditional hierarchical organization, the opportunity to choose your own manager is hard to achieve. But if you move towards the model outlined here, where the roles of strategy and support are separated, then it becomes easy to do.

At Happy people do change their co-ordinators, but not always because they don't get on with them. Some have changed because they became close friends with their co-ordinator. Others have changed because they needed a new challenge and felt another co-ordinator was best placed to give them such a challenge. But there is a simple principle here: the best person to decide who will best support them in development and delivery is the individual concerned.

Questions: *Do your people get any say over who should manage them?*

Could you move towards a situation where they choose their managers?

Notes

1 *Now, Discover Your Strengths*, Marcus Buckingham, p. 6.

2 *HR Review*, 11 November 2009.

Conclusion

It is now more than 50 years since Douglas McGregor set out his Theory X and Theory Y, two opposite approaches to managing people.[1] Under Theory X the assumption is that employees are inherently lazy and will avoid work if they can. This set of beliefs leads naturally to a style of management based on close supervision, levels of approval, and command and control.

In contrast, Theory Y assumes that people are self-motivated and want to do a good job at work. They want to learn and develop and take responsibility. This set of beliefs leads to a very different style of management. It leads to the style outlined in this book.

In 1960, when McGregor published *The Human Side of Enterprise*, there was little evidence to back up the potential of Theory Y. McGregor posed it as a theoretical approach that could change the world of work. Some people took this very seriously. Bill Gore, the founder of WL Gore, is said to have based his new company on seeing what management would be like if it was based on Theory Y. Now a multi-billion-dollar corporation and regularly rated the best company to work for in the UK, it has been described as 'kind of an experiment in management innovation'. WL Gore is one of many that prove the benefits of an approach that I like to call *management as if people mattered*.

It is time to change

We now know how damaging traditional forms of management can be. The difference in productivity between engaged and disengaged employees is dramatic. The evidence is clear that a motivated and engaged workforce is more productive, more committed and far more likely to lead to profitable growth for the company. In contrast, long hours, lack of control over your job and a line manager who does not motivate you can all lead to low productivity, high employee turnover and ill health.

We can create great workplaces. There are plenty of fantastic examples to learn from, whether they be small companies like Happy or major corporations such as John Lewis, WL Gore, Asda or Google. They show the benefits of trusting your people and giving them the freedom, fully supported, to do a great job using their best thinking.

And that is what my company does now. We help organizations to create great places to work in. And it really isn't that hard, as long as you do value your people. So over to you. Whether you are already on this journey or just starting to think about it, what is your next step?

Questions: How much more productive could your organization be if it was a truly great workplace?
What are your first steps to getting there?

Note

1 *The Human Side of Enterprise*, Douglas McGregor (Penguin Books, first published 1960).

The Happy manifesto

In summary these are the simple points that can change workplaces and make them good places to be, and more productive too:

Trust your people
Step out of approval. Instead, pre-approve and focus on supporting your people.

Make your people feel good
Make this the focus of management.

Give freedom within clear guidelines
People want to know what is expected of them. But they want freedom to find the best way to achieve their goals.

Be open and transparent
More information means more people can take responsibility.

Recruit for attitude, train for skill
Instead of qualifications and experience, recruit on attitude and potential ability.

Celebrate mistakes
Create a truly no-blame culture.

Community: create mutual benefit
Have a positive impact on the world and build your organization too.

Love work, get a life
The world, and your job, need you well rested, well nourished and well supported.

Select managers who are good at managing
Make sure your people are supported by somebody who is good at doing that, and find other routes for those whose strengths lie elsewhere. Even better, allow people to choose their own managers.

Play to your strengths
Make sure your people spend most of their time doing what they are best at.

Recommended books

I love management books. Below are some of those that have been key influences on Happy, and on the approach outlined in this book. All are recommended reading.

Relax: A Happy business story, Henry Stewart, Cathy Busani and James Moran (Happy, 2009)

Yes, this is by me and my colleagues. In *Relax* we outline our approach to management in a fictional story. Read how one stressed-out manager discovers an easier way of managing, based on giving people trust and freedom within clear guidelines. Rather similar to what I argue for in this book!

Maverick, Ricardo Semler (Random House, first published 1994)

The book that inspired everything you've read about here. Brazilian businessman Semler explains how he inherited his factory from his father and took it from a workplace where workers were searched each night at the gate to one where they were trusted to set targets, choose managers, organize the workplace and even – in many cases – decide their own salary. Required reading for anybody joining Happy. I have given away over 500 copies.

Now, Discover Your Strengths, Marcus Buckingham (Free Press, 2002)

Here Buckingham outlines the StrengthsFinder philosophy: that it is more effective to get people to play to their strengths than to work on improving areas where they are weak. The book contains a code for the online survey, so each book includes one strengths analysis for a member of your staff. We bought copies for everybody at Happy.

Built to Last: Successful habits of visionary companies, James Collins and Jerry Porras (Random House, 1994)

This book is the result of an extensive academic study comparing companies that succeed in the long term against those that don't. The core message for me was that the companies that succeed in the long term are those that focus on great service, doing the best for the customer and treating both their people and the wider community well – rather than focusing on short-term profit.

Reinventing Management, Professor Julian Birkinshaw (John Wiley, 2010)

New models of management for the 21st century. Packed with inspirational ideas and examples from great companies across the world.

Frontiers of Excellence, Robert Waterman (Nicholas Brealey, 1995)

I prefer this to the more famous *In Search of Excellence*, by Tom Peters and Robert Waterman. Here Waterman gives a range of great examples of how management getting out of the way can lead to true excellence.

The Customer Comes Second, Hal Rosenbluth (William Morrow, 1994)

The message here is simple: treat your people well and they, in turn, will do great things for the customers. Rosenbluth Travel is a multi-billion-dollar company that won the Baldridge award for the best customer service in the entire United States. This book tells their story.

Employees First, Customers Second, Vineet Nayar (Harvard Business School, 2010)

Vineet gives the same message as Rosenbluth but updated for the 21st century and based on his experience in building HCL, a 70,000-strong Indian IT and outsourcing company.

Flight of the Buffalo, James Belasco and Ralph Stayer (Warner Books, 1993)

Buffalo are totally dependent on the herd leader. If the leader is killed, the rest stand around not knowing what to do. In contrast, geese fly in formation, with the leader continually changing. This book, full of great ideas and examples, is about how to make your buffalo fly.

The Servant Leader, James Autry (Crown, 2001)

The concept of servant leadership, originally developed by Robert Greenleaf, is one with many connections to the approaches in this book. The idea is that the role of leaders is not to direct their people, but to serve and support them.

Authentic Business, Neil Crofts (Capstone, 2005)

Neil paints an inspiring picture of another way of doing business, using examples such as Innocent drinks, Yeo Valley yoghurts and Howies clothing. An authentic business, in this definition, has a purpose beyond profit.

How to Win Friends and Influence People, Dale Carnegie (Random House, first published 1936)

Sometimes the classics really are the best. Carnegie teaches age-old truths, such as understanding others, 'walking in their shoes' and relating to their needs.

It's Your Ship, Captain D Michael Abrashoff (Warner, 2000)

People often ask if the management ideas in this book would work in traditional command-and-control organizations such as the military. Abrashoff explains how he used trust and freedom for his people to create the 'best damn ship in the US navy'.

Acknowledgements

This book is based on the experience both of Happy Ltd and of many other companies we have come into contact with. We beg, steal and borrow ideas from wherever we can and encourage you to do the same. I would especially thank all those involved in the Management Today/ Unisys Service Excellence awards, through which I met some fantastic people and companies. And also all those at the Great Place to Work Institute through which, again, I discovered some truly great workplaces.

As noted in the book, the biggest influence on Happy is probably the book *Maverick* by Ricardo Semler. It describes how Ricardo took over a Brazilian manufacturing company called Semco from his father, and transformed it into a business based on trust. I recommend you buy it. Now!

Concepts like 'People work best when they feel good about themselves', 'Celebrate mistakes' and 'Always believing the best' originate from Re-Evaluation Counselling. Find out more at **www.rc.org**.

Other key influences include everybody who works, or has ever worked, at Happy. They are a great bunch of people.

My thanks to Matthew Smith and all at Kogan Page for their help and support with this edition. I am hugely grateful to Stuart Crainer, who gave of his time freely to help me plan, structure and produce this work after I had given up on a first attempt at it. Thank you also to Jenny Boyce of Vertigo Communications, whose knowledge of the publishing world, and considerable patience, made this book possible. If you want to publish a book, she is a great place to start.

And a very special thanks to my wife and children, whose support and inspiration has made possible not just this book but everything I've done at Happy over the last 20 years.

How to contact Happy

Happy Ltd does many things. We train people to use IT, making learning about computers a fun and involving process. We build e-learning, so that people can learn online. And, in our Happy People division, we help organizations create great workplaces.

Happy People is the fastest growing part of the business. We find there is a real hunger and a real eagerness to learn how you make somewhere a great place to work. Most companies now realize that being a great workplace will make them more effective and give them a competitive advantage in the marketplace.

We can help your organization. If it is already doing well, we believe we can make it even more effective. And, if it's a lousy place to work in, we'd love to help you transform it. Contact us now:

Happy People
Cityside House
40 Adler Street
London E1 1EE

020 7375 7300
happy@happy.co.uk
www.happy-people.co.uk

For resources, information and discussion around the Happy Manifesto ideas, check out the website: **www.happymanifesto.com**.

Or contact me directly. I'm at **henry@happy.co.uk** and my mobile phone number is 07870 682442. I'd love to hear what you think of the ideas in this book. Just please don't use these contact details to try to sell me anything!